MIRACLE HUNT

Kimberly L. Alvarado

ISBN: 1977718035
ISBN 13: 9781977718037

DEDICATION

This book of reflection is dedicated to my aunt Camille, whom I have always observed with great attention in order to seek guidance in the areas of faith, patience, and unconditional love. It is her elegance and manner of motion through all the chapters of her own life, in times of celebration and times of trouble, that I have continually admired.

I would also like to thank my daughter Brooke, who encouraged me to continue to write on days when I felt discouraged. Your never-ending support helped me finish an important chapter of my own life, writing a book. To you, Brooke, I'm forever grateful.

And to my husband, Richard, who supported me every step of the way through my first, second, and third manuscripts, never complaining about the leftover dinners and the nights he spent alone while I hovered over the computer.

Thank you to my son, Derek, who always helps me laugh, especially when I need to the most.

And to my daughter, Bailey, I am appreciative of you, for giving me my greatest compliment, when you told me you thought my writing style mirrored that of my favorite inspirational author.

Also, a very special thank you to the editors and Publishing Consultant, along with the entire project team at Amazon for helping me prepare this story for print.

For anyone who has ever met and overcome a challenge.

When my husband and I decided that we had outgrown our lives in the small city where we'd met, married, and almost finished raising our children, we packed up two moving vans, three young adults, and two small pets. It was time to gain new experiences. Life was too short, we agreed. But branching out from my comfort zone revealed some unexpected challenges, causing me to abandon my belief in our plan—more important, in hopefulness and my faith in the future. Almost immediately after our move, as I attempted to redefine the "new" me, I began to receive exactly what I'd prayed for—change. But it wasn't the change that I'd imagined.

Suddenly, I found my thoughts spiraling into the depths of unknown territory. No longer was my future easy and predetermined, like it had been while living in our hometown. There was a new set of tasks placed before me. There was a brand-new path to be walked- new choices to be made. It was a time of trial for me beyond anything I'd ever experienced in my 'simple' life to date.

It took a long time for me to fully grasp a meaningful perspective of the way life's events unfold and how challenges that accompany change often present themselves with a greater purpose.

One year and one horrible hunting accident later, I began to rediscover reasons to have faith in my future again.

CHAPTER 1

"...but those who trust in the LORD will renew their strength; they will soar on wings like eagles; they will walk and not grow weary."

—Isaiah 40:31

I remember the way the dark, frigid air of an early morning felt just before the winter season in the mountains. It's that time just before daylight when the maximum dip in the thermometer numbs your extremities, slowly stiffening them and drawing them into your core. The sting of the icy bite slowly numbs your fingers, your nose, and your toes, working itself slowly up your limbs. That kind of cold kept most everyone indoors, away from the beauty of the forest, for long stretches of bone-chilling months. It's during those early hours of winter mornings that most of the living are still tucked warmly in their beds and the majestic animals of the forest gracefully travel across open fields, seeking their first morning graze before bedding among the bases of ponderosa pine trees just prior to the break of daylight.

Living in northern Arizona for more than thirty years supported an easy recollection of that kind of cold for me, and this season was no different. Like a promise kept, the winter always came
back after the waning of the short mountain summer and the fad-
ing of fall, just after all the colorful leaves had been blown by the
wind from their branches and darkness robbed hours from the
day. When that kind of cold returned every year, it brought with
it hunters and their hopes for success with each freezing sunrise.
In the mind of a hunter, the cold rendered the perfect scenario in
nature for a kill.

This year, however, hunting season in the mountains would be
merely a memory for us. Life's path had taken a new course. My
husband, Richard and I had just sold our home up north. We were
spending the early winter season learning new weather-related
skills in the desert, like how to maintain the proper Ph levels in
our swimming pool, which plants could thrive outdoors during
the winter months and how to maintain proper hydration during
hikes and jogs on desert trails. We were happy to be closer to our
son, who had recently become a college student in a neighboring
city in the metropolis and we had recently registered our girls at
the small public high-school within our new community. Besides
following new opportunities for our children, a primary reason
for leaving the mountains was the fact that Richard had landed a
great job and it was just twenty minutes from our new home (which
in the city, was considered close). I was merely clinging to a 'wish-
list' constructed of what I might like to do with myself now that the
kids were branching off into young adulthood. In reality, everyone
in my family was thriving in our new surroundings-except me. I
was much too quick to regret the new encounters. It was a feeling
of being lost, within myself.

The sky was still black on the morning of Thursday, November
30, when my cousins Preston and Brandon set out with their dad,
my uncle Brian, along the snow-packed winding dirt roads beneath

the San Francisco Peaks for a final opportunity to fill their bull elk tags for the season. Just prior, they had spent the Thanksgiving holiday scouring mile after mile of the forest floor within their northern Arizona unit, hunting together for six previous days. Every season, it was the holiday and the hunt that brought the Hammond boys together. After spending their entire childhood growing up together in Page, Arizona, Preston and Brandon had dispersed to separate Arizona cities to follow college careers and then job opportunities, so they no longer saw each other on a daily basis. When one or more of them drew an elk or deer tag, it was an opportunity for the three to reunite to help one another with the hunt, fulfilling their desire to adventure together outdoors.

The boys had prepared for one final run through their designated unit by loading Uncle Brian's truck in Preston's garage the evening prior. As usual, the boys reminisced over previous hunts, poking fun at each other about who might pull the largest bull from the forest this year, with the vocals of Travis Tritt coming from the speakers in the garage in the background. They piled the necessary supplies into the cab and bed of the white Toyota Tundra, verbally checking off their list, as Uncle Brian made repeated trips into the house to gather more snacks for the cooler.

Preston was tying down a tarp and some straggling contents in the bed of the truck when his wife, Krista, peered around the corner of one door after adding a few turkey sandwiches to the contents of the cooler, propped open in the back seat of the cab. When her eyes met Preston's, her head dropped to one side and her lips tightened into a frowning pucker to express disapproval of her husband's spending another day in the forest. She reminded him of their plans to deck the house for Christmas and how important it was to her that he hang the lights outside so that their son, Jackson, could enjoy his second Christmas season in a colorful "gingerbread" house, as they'd discussed. It wouldn't be long before the next snowstorm would make the task nearly impossible, she reminded him.

Preston paused from arranging his ammunition in the truck just long enough to promise that he'd do it over the upcoming weekend. "It's just this one last day, I promise," he assured her.

Krista nodded in agreement and climbed the garage stairs back into the house. Without further interrupting the preparations in the garage, she scraped leftover cornbread stuffing into a sealed container and finished loading dinner plates into the dishwasher. She was able to tuck away her disappointment by focusing on a planned shopping date with Jackson and my aunt Camille, carrying her thoughts to her Christmas list back in the kitchen and away from outdoor decorating projects until Preston, Brandon, and Uncle Brian returned the next evening.

She reminded herself that hunting season was a common, predetermined occurrence for the Hammond boys. Even before she married Preston, their dating plans were frequently interrupted by fishing tournaments or elk and deer hunts. Nothing had changed since those dating days, and she had to remind herself how attractive she found it that her husband took his outdoor activities seriously. Hunting seasons were highly anticipated by Preston, his dad, and his brother. They were seasons she'd she had learned to accept as a girlfriend and later as Preston's wife. The fact was, hunting season would be part of their lives for many years to come. From the deadline day of applying for tags every summer to the announcement of who'd been drawn and in which unit, a conversation of preparations and scheduling usually paralleled compliments on the rising aroma of stuffed turkey baking in the oven on Thanksgiving.

As a newlywed, Krista became accustomed to that tradition and was frustrated by it only occasionally. Besides, she'd talked herself into believing that this time the hunt was another way for Preston to celebrate the announcement of his upcoming promotion to management within his company. He could go over the details of his recent training in California with his dad and brother during the afternoon hours in the forest, when the guys laid low, alternating snacking and scoping during the hours of sunlight, while the animals were bedded down in the forest. She knew how he was excited for this next career move, and remembered he'd recently expressed that he hoped his new position wouldn't interfere with upcoming hunting seasons. He'd work out those details as they presented themselves, he'd recently told Krista.

Focusing on her own plans for the days that followed, she thought she and two-year-old Jackson could visit Santa at the mall the next morning before they dove into Christmas shopping. Surely, a picture of Jackson on Santa's lap would kick-start a fun holiday conversation when his daddy returned from the hunt.

Dinner with Preston and his family that evening would mark the conclusion of a weeklong Thanksgiving holiday for Krista and a seven-day hunt for the Hammond boys. Afterward, Brandon would head south, back home to the metro Phoenix area, and aunt Camille and uncle Brian would take the northern stretch of highway back to their home in Page, Arizona. Finally, Preston would be home once again, reunited with his wife and young son. With the pressures of obtaining wild game off his mind, the two of them would be able to focus fully on Christmas preparations with Jackson, who seemed to be grasping the excitement of the season through the picture books they had been sharing with him every evening at bedtime.

On the final morning of their hunt, the boys crept silently from the house and backed out of the driveway as snowflakes gently danced across the path of the Tundra's headlight. Krista peeked through the bedroom blinds just as they were leaving. It was well before the sun would ever think about rising. Staring into the darkness at the Tundra's silhouette, she watched as a stream of white mist billowed from the exhaust pipe. Eventually, the two red taillights flickered into the darkness and then disappeared completely as the boys left the neighborhood.

A hunting day like that one must have seemed typical for the trio. After all, my cousins had grown up in the outdoors together. Every season, from the time either boy could pick up a plastic bow and arrow or a toy gun, they hunted and fished with their dad. If it wasn't a rifle, it was a bow and arrow, and if it wasn't winter in the mountains, it was a fishing tournament at Lake Powell in the spring or summer months. The three of them were seasoned in their selection of the best hunting units and the best fishing holes that the states of Arizona and Utah had to offer. As long as they were together in leisure or in sport, the Hammond boys were happy. They depended on one another for support and companionship. It's what this father and his two boys did—through all seasons, year after year, for as long as I could remember. This would be the zillionth time the guys had done this type of hunt. Elk or no elk, the outdoors was their playground. This time, the playing field was Unit 7 East, the sacred land that lies beneath the north side of Arizona's tallest mountain range, the San Francisco Peaks.

Patches of mud and slush barely revealed themselves through the mostly snow-packed, primitive roads just before sunrise that morning as the truck broke off from the highway. Intermittent laughter broke out in the cab of the slow-creeping Tundra. Uncle Brian was behind the wheel, attempting to find a favorable music station on the radio despite the poor reception, and both of my cousins were sprawled out among the extra clothing, binoculars, rope, and sandwiches they'd packed for lunch, along with a grab-and-go first-aid kit. The boys were taking turns expressing their frustration over the absence of quality cell-phone service and Uncle Brian's frequent pit-stop requirements, as their heads rotated slowly from one side of the truck to the other, scouring for movement once the truck left the pavement and continued into the forest. On this particular morning, Brian's shortcomings seemed to be the chosen topic of discussion. At one point during their laughter and broken conversations, Brian blurted out, "I know you think I'm a pain in the ass, but I love you boys anyways!"

With the heater cranked inside the truck and their eyes peeled, the three confirmed among each other that the warm pot of chili my aunt Camille was set to prepare at Preston's house later that evening would be a welcome conclusion to their holiday hunt together, whether a bull produced itself or not. Acknowledging the fact that their tags could remain unfilled was simple reassurance, an expected grace the boys gave themselves and each other to justify their desire to return to the forest next year. The color of winter rendered the truck almost unnoticeable as its camouflaged contents continued creeping along the winding, rutted, snowy dirt roads. Brandon commented that the packed snow would help with their tracking efforts should they be lucky enough to spot fresh elk tracks by daybreak.

Effortlessly, the truck persisted on its wind back to an area familiar to the boys. It was a place where they'd seen elk herds wandering in during a scout the previous summer. As if the animals had known they were safe from rifles during the warm months, they roamed freely among the open fields and timberland floors, and often waded in the watering holes situated sporadically throughout low-lying areas within the forest. There were several ponds the boys could return to that day, time permitting. But at sunrise, their desired destination was near a place called Indian Flats, an area positioned at the base of the north side of the San Francisco Peaks.

Indian Flats is a serene valley with scenic views of the sacred mountains bordering National Forest Service land and the Navajo Indian reservation. Although the valley served as a homesite for the Navajo people many years ago, it was now a large, unoccupied field with a beautiful view of the mountains and no sign of civilization for miles, a place where elk herds were comfortable roaming. The overlooking peaks, which the Navajos deemed the sacred mountains of the west, were the stunning and familiar marker the three needed to track their scouting steps to big herds of game they'd found during previous hunting seasons. The opposite side of the mountain was Preston's home, the place he and Krista bought their first home and a place they decided to raise their family, the city of Flagstaff. It was the same place I had called home for more than three decades.

The Tundra rolled silently along until it paused on a tiny dirt road beneath the historically significant mountain. It stopped near a murky watering hole marked with a crooked and faded Forest Service sign labeled "Road Tank." The boys were familiar with this spot from past experiences, when they'd seen bull elk migrate with herds of cow and young calves toward the murky water for a drink earlier last summer. When the hunters approached the desolate oval pond on foot, searching for tracks, there were none in sight. They all agreed that they wouldn't hunt for long that day. This was partly because they felt a little defeated from six unproductive days in the area already. Besides, there would be plenty of other seasons, they decided.

Without signs of recent activity near the pond, the boys reassumed their positions within the truck and, binoculars in hand, they continued to wind down the ice-covered dirt road as they scanned the familiar hillside for motion. Beams of sunlight were barely beginning to peek through the trees. Each knew this was the time of day when one of them was most likely to spot animal movement along the forest floor. Before the sun had a chance to radiate their shadows, Brian noticed stirring among the branches nearly 200 yards in the distance, there were shadows—of not just one elk, but a few. Uncle Brian inched the truck slowly forward so they could get a better look, and the boys quickly formulated a plan. They would drive to the base of the hill, they whispered, and surprise the herd as it migrated downward. Today might be prosperous after all, Brandon thought.

Hunting is like playing poker in some ways. Depending on the hand your dealt, your luck can change at any minute.

Adrenaline and enthusiasm were building within each of them when the truck finally came to a stop near a fence line at the bottom of the hill. As Brian gently turned off the ignition, the armed hunters silently unlatched the doors, slipped across the seats and dispersed into three separate directions. Quickly yet quietly, the three scattered to assume their staging positions. Uncle Brian stayed closest to the truck, armed with his .300 and knelt down to peer inside his scope. Brandon carried his 7-millimeter rifle and moved almost a hundred yards north along the fence line. Preston, his 7-millimeter also in hand, ran past his brother and traveled the farthest north—to the top of the treed ridge—to view both sides of the hill just in case the animals moved in the opposite direction.

The three used hand signals as they steadied their rifles while traveling across the snow and slush to their assumed stations along the fence line. Preston wasn't yet at the top of the hill when he signaled that a large herd was on the move, coming directly toward the three of them. Steadily migrating towards them was a large group of mostly cow elk and at least one bull. The herd was approaching more rapidly than the boys had initially calculated. They hustled to position themselves in place for a good shot, mostly unaware of each other's positions now, fixated on the sights and sounds of the quickly approaching herd. The sunlight was finally breaking through the tree line and highlighted the elks' reddish-brown hides revealing a silhouette of the rack of one bull traveling gracefully across the snow-covered forest floor toward them.

At first, the herd seemed unaware and uninterested in their camouflaged audience. One at a time, the elk began jumping the fence near the Tundra. But as the animals obtained a scent of human hunters more of them proceeded to trample the fence, penetrating rapidly through the placement of the three hunters. This was it, finally—the opportunity to take down the bull on this frozen, last-chance morning, Brandon remembers. His anticipation brewed and his heartbeat pounded quickly as he focused north through his scope. Seeing Preston briefly in the crosshairs, he continued steadily trailing his gun to the right, in front of his brother, as he followed the bull through his scope. Now spooked, the bull was running for cover within the trees. Seconds later, the sharp sound of a pulled trigger was followed by the sound resembling echoing thunder. It cracked through the trees, Brandon's rifle remained pointed at the broad side of the bull. The piercing sound of the gunshot sent all the animals running for cover. Before he could even lower his rifle to determine if he'd hit the elk, Preston ran a few feet down the hill toward Brandon, his wrist dangling like a ragdoll's. Then, he staggered, yelling in eerie, slow motion, "Brandon, youuu shhh-ot-t meee." Preston fell face down into the snow as his brother's bullet rattled through his torso.

CHAPTER 2

Uncle Brian dropped his rifle and ran through the snow, along the fence line, toward the boys, not believing what he was seeing or hearing. Remarkably, his previous EMT training kept him focused as he motioned and shouted at Brandon, who was standing speechless as he faced his fallen brother. "Get to Preston! I'm getting the truck!" Brian quickly sprinted away to the truck. He returned with the engine racing, crashing through crackling branches and banging against small trees as the truck made its way up the incline toward the confusion. When he reached the boys, Brandon was kneeling over his unconscious brother, who was lying face down and unresponsive. He tried to lift Preston's shoulder to turn him over, hoping this was some sort of sick prank Preston was playing on him. He quickly determined it wasn't. Salty translucent tears dripped from his chin and his nose onto his brother's jacket as he continued to search frantically for signs of breathing.

Brandon and Brian worked together to turn Preston onto his back, revealing a face almost as white as the snow beneath them and a chest bloodied cranberry red. A thick stream of blood pooled from his jacket and followed a path of deep purplish-red down his side, piercing the snow beneath him, verifying the reality of what had just happened. Brandon's thoughts raced. *Oh my God. This cannot be happening.* Then he shouted loud enough for the sacred mountains to hear, "He's breathing!"

Brandon and Brian instinctively lifted Preston, whose limp body felt like it was filled with concrete. Uncle Brian held Preston's arms and Brandon his legs, shuffling the massive weight as rapidly as their adrenaline would allow back to the Tundra. They managed to place Preston in a somewhat upright position in the back seat, to minimize his blood loss, (crucial for a bleeding patient, Brian remembered), with his head resting on the cab's window beneath some crumpled clothing Brian retrieved from the back seat. From the outside window, Preston could be mistaken for a napping passenger, but the inside of the cab told a much different story. Somehow, they had to get help fast! The fact that they were miles from cell-phone service or a paved road haunted them.

As he drove, Brian combed his memory and went over this emergency situation in his head like any other, recollecting his past EMT training. Suddenly, it was time to put what he'd learned during the classes and the tough final exam years ago, in order to help strangers into action, to help his own son. He remembered that it was the gratification of making a positive difference in emergency conditions that prompted him to become officially certified many years ago. He'd become a local part-time volunteer EMT while employed at the power plant when both his boys were still in high school. Volunteering began as sort of a hobby for him, his way of staying involved and busy on nights and weekends in a town that could benefit from his help. For a significant amount of time he helped rescue daredevils on Lake Powell and adventure seeking tourists, who knew little about the dangers of the cliffs or extreme heat in the surrounding areas. It was during his boys' high school years that he turned his interest in helping others into a certified position in his small community. He knew he could be beneficial in the field, because he was a natural at caring for others in dire circumstances.

For as long as he could remember, even prior to any formal training, he'd followed the prompts from his local police scanner around the town of

Page to help the understaffed team of professional EMTs and paramedics who were the first responders to local emergency calls. He was well aware that the units had an inadequate number of professionals to properly service the town of Page and the large reservation surrounding the small town. Additionally, he knew most of the emergency responders on a first-name basis and was sometimes the first to report to a scene, just for the personal satisfaction of assisting them in any way he could. He'd never gotten queasy at the sight of blood and guts that came with this profession. His service in the Vietnam War, as a helicopter pilot, had desensitized him to that long ago. He remembered the adrenaline spikes of night emergency calls and how the abrupt tones crossing the scanner jolted him out of a sound sleep after finishing a full day's work at the power plant. Some nights it was just one call, other nights it was multiple emergencies, only to repeat it all again the next day. There was something motivating about the way emergency responses increased his blood circulation and heart rate, the same affects he experienced while hunting, that kept him motivated in his work. His community service continued for several years. Finally, the pace had become too much for him, and he'd prioritized outdoor time with his boys.

He remained as calm as he could behind the wheel of the Tundra, mentally replaying the basics of his training as he wiped his blood-stained hands onto the tails of his shirt, allowing him to better grip the steering wheel. He took a few deep breaths, trying to calm himself, as everything around him seemed to blur. He'd seen serious situations many times before, he reminded himself, revisiting the car accidents, drowning victims at the lake, and even the suicide call at the familiar address of a friend's house late one night. But those scenarios hadn't taxed his ability to act precisely or challenged his adrenaline like the sight and sound of his own son gasping for breath, when he glanced over his shoulder to the back seat. It affected his ability to think clearly, so he proceeded methodically, not allowing himself to consider the outcome.

Before jumping in, Brandon glanced at the passenger side of the truck, noting the blood smeared on the outside of the passenger door. It resembled a preschoolers finger-painted art project.

The site of it paralyzed him with fear. Brandon joined Preston in the back seat, placed his head near his brother's bloodied chest, and listened for breath sounds, as his dad instructed. Brian turned the truck around to face the snow tracks that had led them to the fence line and pushed the gas pedal to the floorboard, retracing their entrance path into the forest, back toward help.

"You tell me if he stops breathing!" Brian shouted to Brandon, who seemed to suddenly reappear into existence, as he sped through the forest and to the highway. The Tundra was bottoming out on mounds of snow, and the tires slipped, causing the truck to fishtail on the slush and ice. The miles of roadway that they had covered with lighthearted enthusiasm earlier that morning now seemed to be an unending slippery trail, offering only sunlight but no sight of the highway.

"Dad, please don't crash," Brandon pleaded, his voice shaking, as the truck struggled along the rutted, icy dirt road. The sound of the racing engine and the sight of the bouncing speedometer needle added to the anxiety in the cab. With no cell-phone service and at least thirty miles separating the speeding truck from the city limits of Flagstaff, Brian's thumb continued methodically pushing 9-1-1 as he covered one-tenth of a mile at a time, hoping someone would answer. He alternated his attention from his thumb on the cell phone to the boys in the back seat, trying not to look directly at Preston, until the truck's tires eventually met the dry highway. Finally, there was asphalt beneath them.

They sped up to ninety-five miles per hour and headed toward Flagstaff, passing only a handful of cars that seemed to be going at a snail's pace in comparison to the speeding Tundra, as Brandon yelled, "He's still breathing!" With the truck's flashers and headlights beaming, Brian's mind continued to race as quickly as his truck. How would he ever be able to make it all the way into town in time to get help, he wondered?

Then he remembered the small fire station he and the boys had passed on the outskirts of the city on their way out to the hunting unit. It was immediately after they lost sight of that station in the darkness of the early morning when Brian began to request his first pit stop, he remembered. The station probably wasn't fully staffed, he thought, but he was hopeful that someone would be there to help. He shouted out to Brandon that he was driving to the Summit fire station east of Flagstaff. It was the closest facility with emergency personnel, he told Brandon. "Good idea," Brandon agreed, as he continued to place pressure on the chest wound with a blood-saturated flannel shirt. As they neared the site of the fire station, Uncle Brian finally made contact with a 911 operator, who dispatched an ambulance to meet them there.

Once in the parking lot of the remote firehouse, Brian threw the transmission into park and ran to the front entrance of the station, leaving Brandon in the back seat of the idling truck, listening for breath in his brother's lungs. The front entrance was locked, and no one was in sight. Brian pounded on an external metal door on the side of the firehouse, apparently interrupting a meeting taking place inside. "Is anyone here an EMT?" he pleaded to the group.

"I'm a paramedic," someone answered.

The team of emergency responders quickly scurried from their chairs, grabbed a few pieces of equipment, and ran out the side door toward the Tundra. They worked together quickly to move Preston to a gurney, and carried him into the station for intravenous therapy. Endotracheal therapy (in which a tube is placed in the windpipe through the mouth) couldn't be accomplished, because Preston's teeth were clenched tightly together and couldn't be opened. It was apparent to Brian that there wasn't much time to get his son the medical attention he desperately needed to survive.

In hopes of meeting an ambulance, Brian stepped outside. Surveying the parking lot, he saw no sign of an ambulance—only a fire truck, which he reasoned wouldn't be equipped for transport. *Where is it?* he wondered, his mind sprinting in a state of panic. He was unable to think clearly and wondered what he could do next. Fortunately, the Summit fire-station personnel were already in communication with an ambulance, the police, and a trauma team at Flagstaff Medical Center. Within a few moments, which seemed like an eternity to Brian and Brandon, an ambulance with technicians arrived.

They worked feverishly on Preston's nearly lifeless body, preparing him for transfer to the ambulance and finally to the emergency room. Brandon looked on, physically sickened by his blood-soaked hands and the confusion, gaining only a fragment of relief from the sight of paramedics loading his brother into the ambulance. When the two exhausted hunters tried to follow the gurney into the back of the ambulance, they were stopped by the arm of one of the medical responders and instructed to "hang tight" while they waited for police to come and interview them about the accident. The doors closed and locked unsympathetically. The ambulance sped away, leaving Brandon and his dad in the desolate parking lot.

As the echoes of the ambulance's siren faded into the horizon, Brandon's thoughts continued to spin around in his mind like a merry-go-round. Horrified that they couldn't accompany Preston to the hospital, he and his father returned to the fire station's vestibule, huddled together with their heads down, and began to pray out loud. Vocalizing a conversation with God for a few short moments calmed Brian enough to prompt him to call aunt Camille with the news. Brandon listened cautiously, with his eyes closed, to their dreadful conversation.

Brian told Aunt Camille only the basics over the phone. An accident had occurred that morning in the forest, just after the sun came up. Preston was injured, and she should go directly to the Flagstaff Medical Center's emergency room. The seriousness of his voice was enough for her to understand that something terrible had happened. "How bad is he?" she asked, her voice trailing off into a whisper.

Uncle Brian's voice cracked beneath his sobs. "Prepare for the worst."

After about half an hour, a uniformed police officer showed up and summoned Brandon and Uncle Brian outside the fire station for questioning. Step one, they were instructed, was to surrender all weapons in their possession. They impulsively retrieved hunting rifles, a pistol, and some ammunition from among the blood-soaked contents of the truck and laid them on the parking lot pavement. Scattered around the Tundra were binoculars, maps of their hunting unit, and food wrappers, reminders of a morning that had started out so differently.

Worrying and wondering only about Preston's condition, Uncle Brian described, as quickly and precisely as he could, the events of the morning and how they had unfolded into disaster, almost unable to believe it all himself. After taking a few notes, the police officer said that detectives would be asking for more information, and he raced away to catch up to the ambulance. Once again, Brandon and Brian stood waiting.

Everything around them seemed to be a blur. The terror of the seconds after the shot had faded to confusion and was now settling into anxiety and sorrow. The measurement of moments now seemed to reverse to slow motion. What happened in an instant earlier that morning had turned into agonizing, wasted minutes at the fire station. Couldn't these interviews take place at the hospital, they wondered? Uncle Brian and Brandon were beginning to feel like hostages, captives of some sort of nightmare at the remote fire station, wanting nothing more than to be with Preston and Camille at the hospital.

Two detectives in charcoal dress slacks, sharp dress shirts, shiny dress shoes, and black leather jackets coasted into the fire station parking lot in an unmarked sedan. The warmth from their leather gloves remained on their hands as they slowly exited the vehicle and approached the tattered hunters, offering Uncle Brian a hand-shake. One of the detectives routinely revealed his badge. Again, Brian and Brandon were instructed to describe the scenario that had taken place in the forest earlier that morning. One of the detectives took notes as the other listened carefully while Brian meticulously retraced the steps of the morning, beginning with the sunrise. After repeating the events all over again, it was time to return to the scene, they were told, for a reenactment.

The unmarked police car crept cautiously onto the highway, carrying the two detectives in the front seats and my cousin and uncle in the back. They eventually reached the familiar turn onto the snow-packed dirt road that would wind them back toward Indian Flats. Without four-wheel drive, the car crawled and slipped through the snow and slush at a painfully slow pace for the additional fifteen miles on forest roads. Once they reached the base of the hill where the hunters had originally spotted the elk, the four retraced every step of the early-morning hunt.

The process was long and grueling as the detectives, who were improperly dressed for the outdoor conditions, tiptoed through slush and snow to the site where Brandon had taken the shot at the bull elk hours earlier. Brian pointed out some of the details: the trampled fence and the numerous tracks from the herd that had startled the three hunters that morning. A short hike up the hill revealed Preston's 7-millimeter rifle and his binoculars, along with a significant amount of blood scattered across the snow. It was hard for Brandon and Brian to look at the place in the snow where Preston had fallen to the ground. After an additional hour or more of examination, the detectives agreed that the event was an accident, just as my uncle had described in difficult detail at the Summit fire station and again at the accident site.

The ride away from Indian Flats in the back of the detectives' sedan seemed as long and grueling as the trip into the desolate area of the forest. More hours had passed since the catastrophic shot had been fired. Without any updates on Preston's condition, all Brian and Brandon could do was hope that Preston was still breathing. "Please, can you find out if my son is alive?" Uncle Brian pleaded with the detectives from the back seat.

But despite the detectives' repeated efforts to communicate with dispatch and the emergency room, cell-phone service wasn't cooperating in the remote mountainous area. When the unmarked police car finally reached the highway, conversation between dispatch and the detectives resumed and filled the car. Brian recognized the codes they were exchanging, which verified the suspicion of foul play. Brandon wasn't saying anything; his emotions were numb. He stared blankly at the yellow line on the side of the highway. Both of them listened closely as the officers were being instructed by dispatch to bring the emotionally exhausted hunters into the police station for drug and alcohol testing. This procedure would keep them from knowing Preston's condition even longer. Their frustration gave way to tears.

The four of them eventually entered Flagstaff's city limits and were heading to the police station, when the detectives initiated additional conversation with a dispatcher on the other end of the line. "I assure you," explained one of the detectives, "there is no evidence of drugs or alcohol here. These gentlemen need to get to their family. They need to go to Flagstaff Medical Center." Dispatch instructed, "Ten-twelve," for permission to forgo the police-station processing of the two witnesses. This was followed by a "Ten–twenty-four," which Brian recognized as a code for completed assignment. The detective was granted permission to deliver the two of them to the medical center's emergency waiting room.

Brian drew in his shoulders, shortening the back of his neck, and raised his eyes to fixate on the dome light of the car's dark interior, then briefly closed his weary eyes. He was relieved that the detectives were sympathetic to his desire to be with his family, and that his detailed description of the accident scenario was honest and forthcoming, which earned their respect. At last, they would be reunited, although he still knew nothing about Preston's condition. Brian put his arm around Brandon's shoulders. They both clung to each other and to hope that he was still alive.

It must have been around noon, or sometime shortly after, when the fatigued pair of hunters shuffled through the emergency-room doors, nearly collapsing physically and emotionally at the sights and sounds of familiar faces and voices in the crowded waiting room.

That day, my uncle definitely wasn't the same self-assured, confident leader that I'd known him to be all my life. The morning's accident had stolen years from his face and confidence from his stance. I'm certain that morning had also torn a hole through his soul. Looking like a broken stranger, he shuffled his weary body into a chair in the waiting room among the familiar supporters that he hardly seemed to recognize.

Brandon surveyed the faces of those gathered until he found his mother's. It appeared sullen, her eyes swollen with overwhelming anguish. "I'm sorry for what happened. It was an accident," he whispered in her ear as he hugged her, choking on his tears. My aunt hugged him for a very long time. For my aunt, the initial disbelief and shock had succumbed to complete faith and acceptance of reality as Brandon's words pierced her ear. She knew that Brandon was as brokenhearted as she was about the accident.

CHAPTER 3

Learning that Preston was in the hands of a surgical team, still fighting for his life, offered momentary relief for Brandon and Uncle Brian, as I'm sure it did for everyone present at the hospital that late afternoon. The short-term contentment at seeing familiar faces began to fade as the hours of surgery peeled time away from the clock. Brandon continued to sit silently among family and supporters, unable to turn off his thoughts replaying the occurrences of the day. He continually glanced at those gathered in the waiting area, leaning on their elbows and each other for support. His mind continually drifted in and out of reflection of the morning and then to past hunts with his brother.

He thought about their early years, the first archery deer-hunting tag, and how his dad had taken him and Preston to the Kaibab National Forest, where many future hunts followed. As kids, he remembered, it was always either the Kaibab National forest or the units around northern Arizona near Flagstaff where one of them pulled a deer, an elk, or an extended weekend full of memories from the forest. He'd never forgotten the excitement of camping in tents on some of those very first outings, graduating later to a tent trailer that his dad pulled behind his truck or the family van.

Setting up the campsite was as thrilling as hunting for animals in the earliest years. And target practice and pillow fights were just as important to Brandon as the bragging rights of helping to fill Dad's deer tag. Sometimes, he recalled, the weather conditions would be extreme, so the three of them would alternate from camping out to staying in motel rooms, depending on their energy level after a full day of scouting.

It was the winding dirt roads of their past where Brandon and Preston had learned to drive their dad's truck at just ten and twelve years old, their heads barely reaching over the top of the steering wheel. "Do you know your way back to camp?" Uncle Brian would ask, allowing them to take turns returning the truck to their campsite as he walked alongside. It was paradise for the young boys to be able to drive along the unoccupied dirt roads, with an audience of scampering squirrels and ponderosa pine trees, pretending to be Dale Earnhardt or Benny Parsons at the Indy 500, until their dad would return them to the reality of the forest dirt road and motion them back in the direction of the camp.

It was on those trips when the boys were first introduced to campfire dinners—everything and anything in a tinfoil pouch, cooked over the smoldering coals of the fire and smothered in ketchup. Hot cocoa and s'mores many times, a can of beer occasionally in their teen years. There were very few boundaries in the wilderness for the boys. And it was that freedom that made them yearn for more hunting weekends together for decades. It wasn't just one particular season, but the combination of all of their outdoor experiences that had shaped the three of them. Those extended weekends had been bliss for father and sons for as long as Brandon could remember.

It was too late now, he reminded himself, his knuckles holding his forehead up as his fist covered the puffiness of his eyes. The mistake had been made, and there was no way to take it back now. As his thoughts drifted back to the events of the morning,

Brandon confirmed the fact that he never should have pulled the trigger. He recognized the fault a split-second after pulling it, and his conscience kept reminding him of the miscalculation and the catastrophe it had caused. He played the scene over and over in his head, changing the last few seconds before pulling the trigger, until he was weary and mentally broken from the memory of the mistake. It was simple logic, he concluded as he mentally punished himself. The four basic rules of his hunter's safety course had trained him on precisely how to act safely in this exact scenario.

His dad had signed him and Preston up for the hunter's safety course at the local high school when Brandon was just ten years old. He remembered how he anticipated the course and how much fun it was to learn about gun handling, shooting skills, and safety precautions with his big brother in the same classroom. It was sort of like school, but with lessons that he actually found interesting. He would put the newly gained knowledge to good use in the forest with his brother and his dad. He envisioned that after this class, his dad could trust him, and Preston, behind the trigger of a powerful gun. Finally, he remembered, he could earn a hunting tag of his own. He would make his dad proud of him.

Even now, after all those years, he remembered the seriousness of the instructor's words resonating in his ear like it was yesterday, when he defined the basics for his students. Brandon replayed those rules in his head. They were tattooed on his mind:

Rule number one: All guns are always loaded. *(Okay, understood.)*

Rule number two: Never point a gun at anything you do not intend to shoot. (*Agreed. He didn't. It was the monstrous bull elk that he was fixated on, amid the scramble of the large herd.*)

Rule number three: Keep your finger off the trigger until your sights are on your target and you've made a decision to shoot.

And, most important:

Rule number four: Be sure of your target and what is beyond that target.

He couldn't get past rule number four. Not now, not ever. The excitement of seeing and smelling the earthiness of that bull and his masculine rack within the herd overtook his rational reasoning for a split-second. This season, he was going to be the one, out of the three of them, to have the last-minute kill, he thought.

Beating himself up emotionally wasn't going to change anything now, he realized. He needed to refocus his thoughts and energy on his brother. So he prayed silently, among the supporters, that he could stop concentrating on the mistake and asked that Preston would have the ability to overcome adversity, as he had many times before, only never to this extent. This was a big prayer request and he needed big results.

After asking through prayer for reassurance that Preston could overcome this difficulty, he then began to think about previous hunts with happier endings.

One season, he reflected, Preston and his friend Collin had become lost in a snowstorm during a hunt in the Kaibab National Forest. The morning had started out like most of their hunts, up and out of the camp trailer well before the rising sun. This time a storm was on the horizon, so the four guys knew their possibility of filling their tags might be cut short. It was late in the afternoon when heavy clouds quickly rolled in, the skies became gray, and the temperature dropped quickly below freezing. A snowstorm was rapidly approaching. After a long, exhausting morning covering miles of the forest floor on foot, the group had agreed that it was time to call it a day. They were cold, their feet and gloves were wet, and the thought of a warm campfire seemed especially inviting.

Several hours earlier, in the afternoon, Preston had taken a shot at a four-point buck, striking it, but the deer had continued to run. Knowing the importance of finding the wounded deer, Preston and Collin spent the after-noon tracking the blood trail in hopes of securing the animal by nightfall. But the oncoming storm altered their efforts. When the hunters gathered at the truck, they jumped inside, firing up the engine and the heater, and agreed on a short-term plan. After warming up for a few minutes, Preston and Collin would continue to hike toward camp, following the deer's tracks, while Brandon and his dad returned to camp to start a fire and dinner, he remembered.

"We'll see you back at camp," Brian told the boys as they jumped out of the truck and shut the passenger-side door. "Don't be too long," he re-minded the boys. "This storm is moving in quickly." Preston threw the strap of the Savage 110 7-millimeter rifle over his shoulder, nodded, and gave a quick thumbs-up as the truck rolled away slowly through the fast-falling snow. The accumulating storm had quickly covered the tracks and the blood trail of the buck, and the oncoming darkness presented a new challenge for Preston and Collin. After an hour or more of complete darkness, when the two boys had failed to return to camp, Brandon and his dad became wor-ried about their whereabouts and began praying that the storm would let up so that they could return safely.

Brian surveyed the conditions. The snowstorm had dropped nearly six inches of fresh powder on the hood of the truck. And the place where the primitive road lay now blended in with the vast forest floor. Searching for the boys in the truck wasn't an option. He would remain at the camp-base and keep things warm and secure for their arrival. It was something he'd discussed with the boys long ago-should they ever become disconnected from one another in the forest, the campsite was their meeting place. Surely the boys were delayed because they had found the deer, he hoped. Another hunter had probably stopped to assist them with the animal, and they were waiting out the storm in a fellow-hunter's truck. It was common for the Hammond boys to befriend other hunters when they were outdoors. But the forest was dark and cold and quiet. Even with the warmth of the campfire, Brandon remembered the chill of fear he and Brian experienced at the campsite. As more hours passed, this was the first time he feared losing his brother.

After losing sight of the blood drops in the newly fallen snow, Preston and Collin halted their tracking efforts and turned back to where they thought they had remembered the road to camp was. They walked for a couple of miles, greeted by nothing but large snowflakes and darkness. They were growing increasing cold and neither wanted to admit that they were off-track. Eventually they spotted a motor home nestled fairly deep in the ponderosas in the distance. The glowing lights inside drew the lost boys toward its door. They knocked. "You boys lost?" asked a bearded middle-aged man, still wearing his camouflage pants, thermal socks, and fleece sweatshirt. They nodded as the aroma of savory beef stew penetrated the thin layer of ice droplets on their nostrils. Peeling a wet glove from his hand, Preston offered the camper a handshake. The boys, their faces chilled pink, smiled with relief. "Well, come on in and warm up. We'll get you back to your camp."

It was a story the four of them retold for many months following the incident, each of them agreeing not to mention the details of it to my aunt. The dangerous expeditions during their hunts were their secrets alone. The risky undertakings in the forests were partly to blame for their love of hunting.

A warm hand on his shoulder brought Brandon back among the support system in the waiting room that late afternoon. He couldn't help but think of the fact that today wasn't the first time he almost lost his brother. There was the hunt with Collin, when the two of them were lost for a number of hours in the snowstorm. That scenario had ended happily, he rationalized. He needed an ending just like that one all over again. He needed the opportunity to talk to Preston, to tell him that the shot was wrong and completely miscalculated and unintentional.

Realistically, he wouldn't get that opportunity. November 30 was turning into the longest day of Brandon's life, as Preston was transferred to the intensive-care unit following almost five hours of surgery. Looking over his shoulder, Brandon used every ounce of energy he had left to smile in appreciation for the warm touch brushing across his back. He found a fragment of consolation in the familiar voices of family and friends from his tiny hometown, in the rows of waiting-area seats surrounding him, as their conversations went unheard by him and his thoughts drifted over and over again.

George, a good friend of Preston's since childhood, sat next to Brandon and tried to offer words of encouragement. His soft-spoken assurances were appreciated and his presence helped Brandon feel a little better. It was obvious that George, like everyone else, was concerned about Brandon. Together, the two of them went over the events of the morning as more and more hours in the waiting room melted away. George had been at work that morning, he told Brandon, just a few miles down the road from the hospital, when he heard the dreadful news. He had looked at his cell phone during his morning break and noted seven or eight text messages, along with a couple of missed calls, one of them from his cousin in Page. Right away he knew something was wrong. He immediately stepped outside and called his cousin, who told him that Preston had been involved in an accident. She didn't know the details, but news of it was traveling around the town of Page like wildfire. "It was serious," she concluded.

George had talked to Preston earlier in the week and knew he was hunting in the unit just north of Flagstaff, one familiar to him because they had hunted there during past seasons together. He was also mindful of the snowstorm that had moved in and blanketed the forest, making road conditions hazardous throughout the morning. The ice and snow would have made roads especially dangerous in the darkness of the early morning hours, when hunters utilized them to scamper to their units and gain position before daybreak he concluded. His first thought was that Preston and his brother and dad might have been involved in an auto accident on their drive out to their unit that morning. It never crossed his mind that a gunshot might be involved. The Hammonds were experienced hunters.

Moments after hearing that something terrible had happened, George left work and headed to the Flagstaff Medical Center, where he saw the confusion of family and friends just beginning to gather in the emergency waiting room. George arrived long before Brian and Brandon did, so he didn't immediately have any way to find out the details of the accident. It was the conversations that he overheard among family members in the waiting room that convinced him that Preston had been shot. Holding his head in his hands, his heart sank to the floor with everyone else's.

Brandon's only comfort that day came when he thought about some of those past outings with his brother and dad. There was safety and happiness and mental relief in those stories, to which he knew the endings. And as adventurous and dangerous as some of those trips had seemed at the time, they paled compared to today's. Now, all anyone could do was sit and wait and pray.

CHAPTER 4

I was among those clinging to the hope of a miracle in the waiting room in the evening hours following the accident. Like everyone else, I was shaken by the news of what had happened. I'd called my husband at his office earlier that afternoon, after my dad called me with the news, interrupting an otherwise typical day. We'd summoned our son home from his college apartment and our girls from their after-school activities and threw a few suitcases in the trunk of my car before heading north to Flagstaff. I didn't know what to expect when we arrived, and we rehearsed what we might say to my aunt and uncle on the drive up I-17, in the event that Preston had succumbed to his injuries.

When we arrived at the hospital that evening, the sight of all my family's terror-stricken faces felt like a kick in the stomach. How could I possibly respond to Aunt Camille when she thanked us for being there? I knew that, had the roles been reversed and I was sitting in her place, she would have been right where I was standing that moment. Our children are our livelihood—my aunt's personality and mine are paralleled like that. I could hardly speak; the reality of the situation made me speechless. Seeing my family's pain made me feel much worse than the initial phone call, so I focused only on what was directly in front of me, the travel pillow carefully supporting Aunt Camille's neck. I noticed her swollen eyelids and the redness of her chapped nose. And I remember selfishly thinking how fortunate I was not to be sitting where she was that evening. Had I needed to borrow some of my aunt's faith that evening, I'm not sure she would have had any to spare.

Earlier that day, I had been driving toward a vibrant orange sunset and our new home in the desert, having a mental conversation with God regarding my regrets about leaving Flagstaff and moving to the valley. My frustration was whiny and seemed ridiculous to my family. They were enjoying our new lifestyle, so I keep the disappointment to myself as much as I could. I just couldn't seem to find clarity in the positive aspects of our new living arrangement. There wasn't a specific plan for me now that my kids were branching off into their own agendas. Through prayer, I was attempting to sort out the what-ifs and whys as the miles sped by. I was rationalizing the reasons I had agreed to move south in the first place: the opportunities for our kids and the escape of the high country's extended winters. I'd contemplated how the jobs I'd experimented with in my new surroundings weren't the right fit for me, and how I needed help adjusting from my role of full-time parent in my hometown to something that would help me redefine myself in the city. My plan just wasn't falling into place as I'd hoped. I needed clarity for the path of my immediate future.

I kept looking in the rear-view mirror of my life, when what I really needed to do was keep my focus forward, toward my future. I was asking for emotional and spiritual support through my silent words with God when my cell rang. I remember feeling particularly small in comparison to the world and what was happening around me the moment I heard my dad's voice. I was magnetized by the oncoming sunset—and numbed by the words Dad was putting in my ear.

"Hi, Dad." My thoughts immediately broke away from my pathetic plea with God as I focused on the seriousness of my father's voice. "What's up?" I asked, unprepared for the next part of our conversation. Dad skipped the small talk this time and immediately explained that Preston had been shot earlier in the day while hunting up north, near Flagstaff. And before I could even ask, he added, "It doesn't look good."

I was blindsided by his words, and our conversation went silent for many seconds, then a string of ten or twelve questions billowed out of my mouth. He didn't have answers to any of my questions. It was too soon after the accident to predict an outcome, he said. Preston was clinging to life, he explained.

"I'll get there as quickly as possible," I told him before we hung up.

The remainder of that drive home felt like a blur. My thoughts again returned to making deals with God, through prayer. I needed Him to allow my cousin to live, and I would do whatever I needed to do to seal that arrangement.

"God, I'm sorry. I know I haven't clearly trusted Your plan for me. But I'm afraid of my new lifestyle, which is yet to be determined in these new, unfamiliar surroundings. Could you help me understand my purpose here? Would you help my cousin Preston? Can you comfort him and his family? Please don't let him die. They need him. Don't let them down— there's so much left for him to do here."

My lack of concentration on the road caused me to believe that my car knew its way home that late afternoon because I don't remember traveling past any familiar milestones the rest of the way. My discussion with God was interrupted by the clicking of the turn signal as I pulled into my garage. When the door lowered behind me, I sat in my car in the complete darkness for a few moments, wishing I could start that morning over again and force the day to evolve differently. I could almost feel that same wish radiating from the Hammonds miles away in the emergency room in Flagstaff. We needed to get there-quickly.

CHAPTER 5

Back at Flagstaff Medical Center, the "golden hour" had long passed. Unspoken condolences were exchanged through glances among us in the waiting room. There wasn't much to say among us. I assumed our thoughts were all teetering on the what-ifs. It was as if we were unanimously anticipating the reality but clinging to the slightest possibility that something extraordinary would happen behind the closed doors of the intensive-care unit. No one would doubt that those chances were microscopic, however.

More realistically, we were all there to console Uncle Brian, Aunt Camille, my cousin Brandon, Preston's wife, Krista, and their precious little Jackson at a moment's notice when a doctor might appear in the doorway to say that he'd done all he could to save Preston's life. At some point during those fragile hours of the first night, the Hammonds brought Preston's best friend, Collin, to the area where Preston was being monitored and observed. Collin stood over Preston and sobbed as he looked at the tubes protruding everywhere from his friend's broken body. He held Preston's hand and talked about the plans he had made for a future hunting trip, and he gave Preston his finest "backyard fighting" speech. He was serious about his demand to survive, he told his best friend.

This time it was going to be the fight for his life, but he knew if anyone could do it, Preston could.

Collin had been friends with Preston since the two of them were in elementary school. The boys had grown up almost neighbors on First Avenue, with only eight houses separating theirs. They were originally introduced by their moms, who visited on the sidewalk in front of their houses on warm spring afternoons. There were birthday parties, dirt bikes to ride, walks to school, and desert hikes that became the foundation of their friendship in the early years. He fondly remembered transforming an empty lot between their houses into a baseball field and then gathering up as many neighborhood boys and their brothers to fill two teams. He couldn't forget the celebration of winning the Little League championship on the Astros team one year, or the many hunts with Preston, his dad, and his brother in the Kaibab National Forest, including the one when he and Preston became lost in the snowstorm. Those were some of the best experiences he'd had growing up.

In their high school years, Collin and Preston wore the same black and red jerseys when they played high school baseball for the Page Sand Devils. Traveling together for away games and the sometimes grueling after-school practice sessions strengthened the bonds of their maturing friendship. Collin remembered Preston as the one who would always initiate the social activities. He frequently searched for opportunities to gather the group, their buddy George included, to attend a concert, fish in a local tournament, or chase girls together. That kind of fun continued until the last school bell rang, sending the three high-school graduates into college studies together at Yavapai Community College and, later, Northern Arizona University. Eventually, the three boys went their separate ways, as jobs and weddings sent them straight into adulthood. Preston, he remembered, always remained the glue that occasionally reunited them, long after their lives were complicated by jobs and everyday life. He wished he was meeting Preston today for another chance to reconnect or brag about their recent hunting tag fulfillment.

Collin had been tending to some yard work that morning at his home in Page, when he received a call from a high-school friend who asked him if he'd heard about Preston's accident. He dropped the shears he was using to trim some overgrown shrubs around the front of his house. He pulled himself onto the first step of the porch and stared at the ground. He initially just sat there, and then he cried uncontrollably as his wife guided him back into the house. Within several moments after hearing about the accident, Collin and his wife filled their car with gasoline and headed north, directly into the snow flurries, and they approached the Flagstaff Medical Center not knowing what condition they'd find Preston in when they arrived.

As I observed the faces of those congregated around the Hammonds, and the ones of those trickling in and out of the waiting area, I couldn't help but feel the strength radiating from the circle of supporters. Every person gathered in that waiting room was linked to Preston, their connection woven into his history through past experiences with him and his grieving family. My thoughts began to wander.

As more hours passed and the wait continued, I remembered the small town of Page, Arizona, as the home to my cousin's family, as it had been mine, and its representation of support in the waiting room that afternoon and evening. It was construction jobs at the Navajo Generating Station that had brought my future Uncle Brian's family to Page (as it had my family and many of our extended families). The small town must have seemed safe and welcoming to Brian after returning from his tour in the Vietnam War in 1973. Page was a place where most families felt comfortable leaving their front doors unlocked. The atmosphere was quite a contrast from the sounds of explosions and gunfire that he'd been exposed to while at war. After he left the service, Brian lived with his parents in Page and worked temporarily as a guide on the Colorado River. But river work was seasonal, so when Salt River Project, our public power utility company, held testing that same year, Brian scored high enough to secure a plant operator's position at the Navajo Generating Station, a stable career in that small community.

I thought about how jobs and circumstances were why my family had then moved away from Page, as had many branches of our family tree. The completion of construction of the power plant was concluded in the mid-seventies, marking the time for many of us to move on to other places for work. Frequent moves were part of a lifestyle families in construction work learned to adapted to. My dad did his best to avoid the frequent relocations and strategized a central Arizona location for our family-which landed us more permanently in Flagstaff. During the following years, we had left Aunt Camille, Uncle Brian, Brandon, and Preston in that quaint little spot on the map, where they continued to create relationships and memories with those who were now gathered to console one another.

Even Preston had left Page in recent years, after high school. Like many of his friends and classmates, he needed to branch out from a place that didn't have much to offer young adults who weren't already established at the power plant. He headed to college in the northern part of the state, returning to his hometown frequently to visit family and friends, and then to marry his sweetheart from high school, Krista. Even though he no longer lived in Page, my cousin's roots remained deeply embedded, and were well represented that evening in the hospital waiting room by the small town that had built him.

CHAPTER 6

SMALL TOWN ROOTS

Our family's original connection to Page, Arizona, comes from a much happier season. Maybe it all begins with an understanding of our background. Our family tree, at least in my lifetime, as with my cousin Preston's, begins with our grandparents Myron and Gloria, whom us grandkids called Mim and Pip. Our grandparents were eternal optimists when it came to moving forward in life, and their strong faith carried them through the ups and downs I'd watched them handle over and over while growing up. The two of them migrated to Page in the early 1970s, when my aunt Camille was in high school, for the construction work at the Navajo Generating Station. Soon thereafter, my parents relocated to Page as well, placing me within the comfortable surroundings of extended family and small-town living.

Camille had entered her freshman year at Page High School during the time when the Watergate hearings began in the US Senate, Billie Jean King was dominating tennis matches around the country, and American Graffiti—in which George Lucas brought Americans drag racing through the end of a quintessential precollege summer vacation—was nominated for five Oscars. It was a simpler time for our nation, and certainly a simpler time for her. She was flourishing in her new school, seemingly never frightened by change, like I was. As her high-school years advanced, so did her popularity. She became a member of the varsity cheerleading squad, upheld good report cards and secured a job, for spending money, at the local fast-food fried chicken restaurant. She'd readily adapted to change. Arizona was across the nation from her previous playing field. And the set of circumstances that got her to the next chapter as a young adult came easily, as it did for Mim and Pip, because of her faith in moving forward.

Mim and Pip's story of relocation to northern Arizona began numerous miles away and many decades prior to Preston's accident, across the country in what now seems to me like another lifetime.

My grandparents journey, from the east to the west coast:

Myron and Gloria Fountain were born and raised and got married in a small northeastern town outside of Detroit, Michigan. In 1945, after World War II, my mother, Victory Joy, was born. She was the first of five children. Following my mom were her four siblings, my aunt Gayla, uncle Brian Fountain, aunt Camille, and uncle Leslie. As the days and months melted into years, the five "stairstep" toddlers grew into children and then young adults in a small town called South Rockwood. As did most families on their block, Myron, Gloria, and their children developed into a typical Catholic family in suburban America during the late 1940s and early 1950s.

The little I know about my grandparents' lives in Michigan was told to me by my mom, Victory. Pip, who had been a stellar member of his high-school swim team, married his high-school sweetheart, Gloria Chamberlain, after returning from World War II and worked for many years in a factory. They raised their five children in a pretty, well-kept, two-story Michigan home whose front yard was accented by a giant black walnut tree. Their block was the picture of the American dream and the ideal playground for the Fountain children for many contented years.

The way my mom remembers her life growing up in Rockwood is probably similar to the recollections of most families from those years, a time when Americans were happy to put the war behind them. In fact, the Fountain family marched to the beat of the same relatively simple drum for decades, with only a couple of notable setbacks. One was the extreme fever that sent their youngest, my uncle Leslie, into an episode of convulsions when he was a toddler. Another was the unexpected medical emergency that sent my aunt Gayla into a comatose state, when she narrowly escaped death. My grandmother's intuition led her to direct Pip to drive them to the hospital that day after a doctor visit. It wasn't the flu; it was juvenile diabetes.

Indeed, the Fountain family, with roots in the compact town, followed its customary pattern of life for many years. So, according to tradition, my Mim and Pip would have repeated the monotonous template, living and dying in the same spot, had they remained complacent.

Instead, as time chipped away at their Michigan years, their firstborn, my mother, graduated from high school and moved across the country to California, marrying my dad shortly thereafter. Soon Pip agreed, with a great deal of convincing from Mim, that hometown winters in South Rockwood were too cold and too long. Without hesitation, the comfortable family-home that my grandparents worked hard to obtain went up for sale. I never really questioned how all of their belongings got across the country or how Pip was brave enough to quit his job and leave his native state without a solid plan; I just know that he and Mim made up their minds one summer to leave, and were optimistic about beginning a new chapter in their lives "out west." It must have been faith in the good Lord and his positive attitude that guided Pip, four kids, and all of the camping equipment necessary to get them to the beaches of the West Coast—one campsite at a time.

A particular reflection from my aunt Camille, about that move to California, is one of my favorites:

> *Pip had arranged for Mim to fly from Michigan to California via a commercial airline, because she'd recently undergone knee surgery and couldn't manage the almost two-thousand-mile road trip in a station wagon with four kids and a happy-go-lucky husband. Pip, the unemployed eternal optimist, and his precious cargo camped through the states of Ohio, Illinois, Nebraska, Colorado, and Utah before reaching their new home in Orange County, California.*

I can almost hear her muffled chuckles as Camille describes the seating arrangement in the station wagon across the endless stretches of highway as it crawled west along Route 66. Her oldest siblings, she remembered, occupied the front bench seat and operated the radio dial next to Pip. Meanwhile, the younger brothers and sisters alternated around in the back, bench seats. This meant that Camille's position, along with that of her younger brother Leslie's, was often horizontal in the rear luggage area, among the contents of necessary camping equipment and anything else that couldn't be tied to the top of the family wagon.

By day, she drew sunflowers and stick figures in the dust that collected on the windows of the station wagon as it consumed the miles of highway leading to their next routed stopping point. When darkness fell, she and her brother glanced into the heavens, searching for planets and star constellations from an obscured view out the back window. The lengthy stretches of days and nights traveling the highways weren't without incident, however. She didn't remember which state or which hundred-thousandth pit stop, but somewhere during the journey, Camille had come out of the gas-station restroom to an empty parking lot. She'd been forgotten! But she was alone only until the family head count (maybe forty or fifty miles down the road) took place in the station wagon. She remembered the salty tears rolling down her sweaty cheeks and the distress she felt as the store clerk held her hand while they waited near the gasoline pump for her apologetic father to return for her in the overpacked station wagon.

California remained my aunt and grandparents' home until Arizona called with a new opportunity in the construction field, specifically the construction of the Navajo Generating Station, for Pip.

CHAPTER 7

I know she would have taken back that fear in an instant. Camille would have easily traded the fear of being left behind by her family as a child for the distress she felt in the waiting room at the Flagstaff Medical Center that evening. Unfortunately, that exchange of emotions wasn't possible. By no choice of her own, she'd been pulled into this dire set of circumstances. Yet, as expected, she remained calm and focused in thought, knowing that the situation was way beyond the limits of her control. She would depend entirely upon her faith and her family to get her through what was happening.

Many hours had passed since Preston's lifeless body had been rushed through the emergency-room doors and into surgery. Now, my cousin Brandon and my uncle Brian were clinging to the hope that they had acted quickly and sufficiently enough in the moments just after the shot was fired to make a difference in Preston's battle against death. Questions continually formed in Brian's mind as the waiting room filled and the night continued. Had his past EMT training aided in Preston's survival to this point? He silently commended himself that he remembered it was important to keep a gunshot wound elevated and the patient positioned with the wound side down to keep him from choking to death on his own blood. One for him, he thought. How did he remember anything at all? He hadn't ever felt as panicked- not on an emergency call, nor in Vietnam, not ever.

And the chosen route out of the forest—it proved to be the *best* one, he concluded. Had he and Brandon decided to circle the mountain base in the opposite direction, it would have brought them to Highway 180, closest to the northwest end of the city. The highway may have been closer in proximity to civilization, he reminded himself, but it was definitely farther from medical assistance, and that road probably would have been more highly populated with travelers going to and from the Grand Canyon. He didn't remember why they initially chose to return to the same path that had brought them to the northern base of the mountains, but now established that the route had been the *right* one. And the freezing temperatures that made it seemingly harder to maneuver the truck to the dry highway for assistance proved helpful in terms of slowing Preston's blood loss and some of the internal swelling during the time of transport from the hunting site to the Summit fire station. Despite the terrible circumstances he was facing, he needed reassurance within himself that he'd done everything he could to help save his son's life.

Behind the closed doors of the emergency room, Preston's life was in the hands of a trauma team led by Dr. Mark Donnelly. Dr. Donnelly was a well-trained and highly respected member of FMC's board of directors and surgical team who specialized in vascular and trauma surgery and had more than a decade of experience in his field. If anyone could have been hand-selected to be on duty in the emergency and operating room that day by the Hammond family, it would have been Mark Donnelly.

He and his team worked feverishly to examine Preston's non-responsive body. Preston's body temperature had dropped to 35.6

degrees on arrival. Besides being in a state of hypothermia (and the obvious bullet wound in his chest), he was hemodynamically unstable— which meant his blood wasn't circulating properly. His teeth were still clenched tightly together, and his pupils were fixed and dilated, an indicator of injury to the brain. There was no movement to his body whatsoever. The examining doctors noted that there was no evidence of an exit site; the bullet, they later found, had lodged in the soft tissue of his back. In addition, his forearm had been pierced by the bullet also. There appeared to be internal bleeding and insufficient breathing. He had no obvious pulse anywhere, other than a weak one in his groin area, and the examining team had doubts that he could be saved. During the brief prep for surgery and observation period in the ER, Preston had even developed an abnormal heart rhythm in the large chamber of the heart, and tachycardia was depriving his organs and tissues of oxygen. At this point, every second was significant, and any miscalculation meant the difference between life and death.

Within minutes of the initial examination, Preston was prepped and taken into the operating room, where a tracheal intubation was performed. The right chest cavity was opened through a lengthy lateral incision. His chest was filled with blood. The bullet was recovered, and a portion of his hemorrhaging right lung was removed. A short time into the surgical process, Preston became increasingly difficult to ventilate. He developed multiorgan system failure, sending his heart into cardiac arrest. Immediately, the surgical team began to perform open cardiac massage, but his heart refused to regain a rhythm on its own. The expert team of doctors worked frantically to regain his heart function, using electrical cardioversion to try to maintain a normal beating rhythm. Once started, it would shut-down again. Preston's heart was shocked three times on the operating table that day. The third and final try was successful! It had been nearly five hours of surgery, and finally he developed a good cardiac rhythm.

Assisting Dr. Donnelly with the surgery was Dr. Randall, who examined the second bullet wound to Preston's right wrist, which had been fractured by the bullet. It clearly exhibited an exit wound. It was determined that the bullet had first pierced the right wrist before it entered his chest. This could have been the reason the bullet had not exploded or exited his back. Dr. Randall determined that the gunshot wound to the wrist was secondary to Preston's critical thoracic trauma, so the wrist wound was merely irrigated and splinted. It could be operated on at a later time, depending on Preston's ability to survive.

After more than four and a half hours of surgery and at least an additional hour of observation post surgery, Dr. Donnelly noted with astonishment that his patient exhibited reasonable neurological function during the early postoperative period. After documenting the details of surgery and postoperative observation, he made his way to the darkened waiting area and the exhausted figures of those left waiting with Aunt Camille, Uncle Brian, Brandon, and Krista. The tone of Dr. Donnelly's voice was unwavering, as he was careful not to instill any false hope about survival, despite the immediate success of stabilizing Preston's vitals. In reality, he explained, Preston's condition was extremely critical, and his breaths could only be accounted for one minute at a time. He refused to look any further than that into Preston's future, he told the Hammonds.

Shortly after this postsurgical meeting, Dr. Donnelly pulled my aunt and uncle away from everyone else and told them that Preston might not make it through the night. He agreed with Camille that it was an appropriate time for last rites to be given to his critically damaged patient. Father Lou Franz administered those rites that night at Preston's bedside as he lay unresponsive, surrounded by his immediate family. Shortly after saying their possibly forever good-byes, Father Lou, Camille, Brian, Krista, and Brandon retreated to the hospital's chapel to hold on to each other and pray together. Out loud, the brokenhearted family, minus one of its essential pieces, recited the Lord's Prayer and the Hail Mary, each adding personal prayers for their loved one's healing.

Darkness clung to those in the waiting room, where a number of hours earlier, reality had turned an adventurous morning in the forest into long, silent hours of night in the grief-stricken medical center. The frigid cold had slowed the movement around the waiting area, numbing the minds of the few left there that first night. Before situating himself on a couple of chairs pulled together, Brandon remembered, above everything else, the tone of Dr. Donnelly's voice when he initially reported stabilization to the family, which had never hinted at a fragment of hope after the surgery, and how excruciating that solemnity had been for him to hear.

Hours later, well into the middle of the night, Dr. Donnelly appeared among the sleepers sprawled over chairs and on the floor, reporting that Preston was not yet out of imminent danger and that things weren't going well in the ICU. In their minds, my relatives could be summoned to Preston's bedside at any moment. The sleepless moments continued and there was nothing to say amongst them.

But several more hours passed, and the sun began to peek through the windows of the somber waiting area, its brightness piercing Brandon's heavy eyelids. Somehow, there was ongoing life to be thankful for. By seven thirty that morning, the first twenty-four hours following the accident had passed. Then, twenty-four more hours crept by, turning slowly into forty-eight and then seventy-two. For several more nights my aunt, my cousin, and my uncle propped themselves against chairs and each other, covering themselves with coats and lap blankets as they waited and continually thanked God for each additional hour added to Preston's life.

Preston was placed in a medically induced coma immediately following his initial surgery, where he remained completely unresponsive and unaware of his surroundings. He was now in a quiet, dimly lit room in the ICU with tubes and needles protruding from his body and a ventilator assisting his every breath. His wife, parents, and brother could finally sit by his bedside in short intervals, before returning to the waiting area, where family and friends continually gathered to talk about the incident and offer their support.

As I observed Brandon during the initial hours and days following the accident, I wondered what was going through his mind. He hardly said anything. He barely looked directly at any of us, even at Dr. Donnelly. He was clearly experiencing grief, distress, and disbelief. Without a doubt, his life had suddenly taken a drastic turn from simple to complex. Although I couldn't completely read his thoughts, it was evident he was in deep thought, often looking upward as he prayed. I wondered if his prayers were being heard. Recently, I'd questioned the validity of mine. "Please hear him," I remember saying in my mind.

Over the next few days, Camille and Brian divided their concern between their two sons, and Krista divided her emotions between her husband's condition and the needs of her son, Jackson. The Hammonds were clearly heartbroken, and were displaying varying thoughts and concerns for one another. Besides keeping a round-the-clock bedside vigil for Preston, the Hammonds continued to keep a watchful eye on Brandon to make sure he didn't slip deeper into depression. The tragic miscalculated shot at a passing elk had made a quiet but easygoing man into a quieter, more introverted one. Day after day, more than ever, his words were fewer, and his thoughts were difficult to read.

CHAPTER 8

*I*n his earlier years, Brandon had been accident-prone yet seemingly invincible. The unwaveringly carefree youngster that I'd watched grow up
over the years was now a subdued adult hoping that his brother would be
invincible too. Brandon had slighted his way out of potentially dangerous
situations many times as a young boy. Aunt Camille remembered when
she nurtured her youngest adventure seeker with ice packs and children's
Tylenol, and they even had a few trips to the emergency room for sprains,
ear infections, and, once, a golf ball–sized goose egg on his forehead after
he'd jumped off a bed, landing on his head at Mim's house. If there was
a chance to experience 'what would happen ifs,' Brandon would give it a
try. I still cringe when I think about her recollection of the incident when
Brandon clipped a hot curling iron onto his index finger while at a babysit-
ter's house. The blister that formed filled with liquid, creating a huge bubble
that required medical attention. He lost the nail on that finger—and my
aunt some sleep—yet, like many young boys his age, no setback would ever
derail his interest in adventure or affected his ability to recover.

In grade school, Brandon's playground during late afternoons and on
weekends was the desert that surrounded his neighborhood. He and his
buddies spent many afternoons building jumps for their bikes from plywood
and bricks gathered from empty lots near their homes. They gathered rocks

with unusual shapes to add to last summer's collections, and caught lizards for endless hours in the open spaces around their homes. It wasn't unusual for the grade-schooler to return home any given evening before dinner with a jug full of squirming reptiles or a jar full of scorpions he'd collected in the desert. More than a few times, he'd show up a few minutes late to church on a Saturday evening on his bike or scooter, his dirt-streaked face prompting disappointed sighs from his parents (who had spent an hour prior to the service searching for him). But despite Brandon's independence and love of risky entertainment with his buddies, he let his mom domesticate him just enough to introduce him to the simple pleasures of doing for others and connecting to the community.

Instant Jell-O chocolate pudding was the secret ingredient in Brandon's "homemade" chocolate pie. He carried his' masterpiece' concoction from the parking lot, across the grass in city park, all by himself, and positioned it in the center of the judge's table among the other entries. The pie-baking contest across from his elementary school one summer weekend had been Camille's idea. She enjoyed participating in such events and encouraged her boys to join in. It didn't take much convincing from my aunt for this one. Chocolate was his favorite, probably everyone's he thought, and he held little doubt that he'd have any trouble convincing the judges his pie should prevail. This time, the handful of participants also included a local restaurant owner and three ladies from a neighboring church. I remember the tightened lips and raised eyebrows of the runners-up when Brandon was declared the first-place winner that afternoon. Undoubtedly, the contestants had spent significant time and effort perfecting the recipes of their confection entries. Apparently, the judges appreciated youth participation. We looked on from the background as Brandon moved forward toward the judges to proudly claimed his prize. He didn't notice the onlooking stares and never flinched at the fact that he was the only non-adult participant. We chuckled all the way back to Aunt Camille's house as Brandon waved his blue ribbon out the back window of the family minivan, watching the wind catch its streamer tails as a partially-dried glob of chocolate oozed from the side of his mouth. For the moments it took to drive back to their home, he was a winner in every sense of the word. But his first-place award in the community contest was quickly forgotten when we pulled into the driveway. Brandon would leave the remains of the chocolate pie, along with the winning ribbon, on the backseat and immediately jump on his bike to disappear on his next desert adventure.

He had grown up in the 1990s, and modern technology hadn't yet affected his small town. Before technology became the main focus, a young teenager often had to design his own kind of entertainment and keeping himself busy never seemed to be an issue. If he and his buddies weren't exploring the desert on their dirt bikes or four wheeling in one of their dad's trucks, they were fishing from the sides of the family boat with his parents or those of a friend on Lake Powell. Most often in recreation, Brandon had a separate group of buddies from his brother's, who were older. But occasionally, both Hammond boys would incorporate adventure with neighboring fathers for fishing or nighttime hunting activities like "bunny busting" which involved 'boy's and dad's only' trips into the desert or wilderness. Those years were when the Hammond boys were introduced to .22-caliber rifles and the basic concepts of hunting rabbits and coyotes. Little did the boys know at the time, but hunting and the outdoors would connect them to so many lasting friendships and relationships in their futures.

CHAPTER 9

Preston's condition continued to be grave and unstable, and the Hammonds continued to try to answer the questions of concerned visitors—over and over, to the best of their ability. Preston's fate was clearly unknown, and that fact was frustrating, and my aunt and uncle were hiding the fact that Dr. Donnelly told them that Preston could be mentally handicapped from the extreme loss of blood he'd experienced. Talk of the what-ifs further fatigued Camille, Brian, Brandon, and Krista. Everyone involved was looking for answers that just weren't possible for the doctors to provide.

By December 3, many of the visitors who had initially filled the hallways and waiting area of the Flagstaff Medical Center had gone back to their own schedules and routines, returning for visits during the evenings and weekends. I was one of them. I had returned to the Phoenix suburbs, leaving my cousin and his family with the dreadful task of observing Preston's fight for survival. That I couldn't support them in Flagstaff every day was difficult for me; I felt guilty. I needed a way to stay close to the situation. It didn't seem appropriate for me to merely call every day. I knew I couldn't change Preston's circumstances, but it was important to me to try to make a positive difference somehow. I craved a bigger connection, to let my aunt and uncle know that I truly cared about what they were going through.

After a bit of soul-searching and then some research on the Internet, I found and registered on CaringBridge, a personal-health website. The site would allow me to open a journal-type display, dedicated to my cousin and could outline the details of the accident while encouraging supporters to add their own personal messages as they followed along each day for updates on Preston's medical journey. Camille and Brian appreciated the idea of it. The site would also allow them to reach out to those who couldn't be at the hospital on a daily basis. Their laptop computer could keep them connected to friends and family and it became their means of support through the grueling days to follow. After speaking on the phone with one of the Hammonds every evening, my plan was to write a paragraph or two about Preston's care and progress. The newly-designed site helped channel my energy, with words and in-spiration for everyone close to my cousin. It was my way of helping from a distance, and it eased my anguish and feeling of displace-ment after our recent move from Flagstaff.

The site became a documented space for "praying out loud" for everyone who wanted to write to Preston personally, and the messages could be read to him by his parents as he fought for sur-vival. In a time before Facebook, facetiming, and cell phones with cameras, the website proved therapeutic for my cousin's family and for well-wishers, who could post comments and messages of inspi-ration for healing. It also relieved the stress of having to repeat reports to concerned visitors, so the Hammond family could focus fully on Preston and his physical needs. From the moment I reg-istered on the site, it felt like I'd opened some sort of hotline to heaven, as contributors began to pour out encouragement to the Hammonds and each other through daily prayers and reflections.

I initiated the CaringBridge journal for my cousin with this short message:

On November 30, a tragic hunting accident happened to a loving family member, Preston Hammond, while he was hunting with his dad and brother. Preston was accidentally and critically wounded. He is courageously fighting for his life.

By the next morning, messages of concern began popping up on the site. It was the connection to my cousin that I needed. I think every one of us close to him needed an outlet to express our apprehension.

By December 4, Ty and Angela's was among more than a dozen messages of inspiration written to Preston and his family on CaringBridge:

Preston and Family,

Wow, does God have a plan for you! Your life is a constant miracle and we trust that God will use you and your family in extraordinary ways! We continue to lift you up in our prayers daily. Find comfort in one of our favorite verses:

"For I know the plans I have for you," declares the Lord, "plans to prosper you and not to harm you, plans to give you hope and a future." Lean on the promises of God, he never fails!"

Jeremiah 29:11

Ty and Angela—Prescott, AZ

Another entry on the site that day was a message from Jason and Cami, friends in Colorado, encouraging the Hammonds and Preston to continue their fight. I loved the messages I was reading. I could hear echoes of Brian reading the passage to Krista and Camille and Brandon and Preston. Jason and Cami's message summed up the initial hours and days in the ICU:

> These tests in life are only dealt to the strong, the ones who can handle them. We know how strong your family is. Preston, we know for sure that you can take on this challenge and we know you won't quit until the challenge is overcome. Fly like an Eagle buddy. Our love and prayers.

That first weekend, like many family members and friends, I returned to Flagstaff Medical Center to circulate among the rotation of visitors in the waiting area. I could sense that it was comforting for the Hammonds to have shoulders to lean on, to help fill the endless hours in their temporary home. They had recently been moved to a larger, more private waiting area, which better accommodated the numerous visitors as well as the sleeping needs of the family.

I recall catching a few moments of conversation with Aunt Camille, Krista, and Brandon before taking my turn to briefly visit Preston. Visiting Preston meant a quick sweep through the sterile, serene room where he lay in a coma, attached to life support by tubes and needles. We could talk to him, touch his swollen hands, and tell him that we loved him, but there was absolutely no response. I wasn't sure he knew what I said, but I told him that he looked strong and that we all needed him to take his time to heal, but that we expected him to come back to us. Within the first week in the ICU, the miracle of Preston's revival became the quest for his survival, and it was evident that it would take everything within him to overcome his critical situation.

It wasn't until the fifth day in acute care when Krista, Brian, Camille, and Brandon were allowed to spend longer intervals by Preston's bedside. It was small victories at first—there was an eye flutter on December 4 —progress that I was anxious to report on CaringBridge. Any bit of information, however minor, seemed to keep many friends and family supporters hopeful for his survival.

As he geared up for a journey of unknown length at Flagstaff Medical Center, Uncle Brian found his position at Preston's bedside, in a worn recliner chair, for what was to become a long and tedious road ahead. He spent nearly every hour of every day assisting the nurses with anything he could in regard to Preston's care. The little things, like changing messy bedsheets, gowns, and surgical-gauze bandages, helped my uncle feel that he was doing something to aid in Preston's recovery process, while keeping his mind off his remorse over that fateful November morning. He was deputized to work in the intensive care unit for as long as he was needed, and the nurses appreciated his assistance greatly.

Every day, Brian spent a considerable amount of time reading the local newspaper aloud to Preston. The hometown happenings kept him connected to what was going on around the city, outside the walls of the hospital, a reminder that life was continuing its forward motion. He hoped Preston was absorbing some of the information he shared with him. At the very least, Preston seemed at ease with the calmness in my uncle's voice, brought on by the words read aloud to him. Brian's tone brought a peacefulness familiar to my cousin to the quiet space within his room. Preston's comfort level was measured by the steadiness of the whirring overhead monitors attached to the machines keeping him alive.

After covering all pages of the news, Brian would switch his focus to trivia questions, pausing for a response, and then eventually filling in the answer himself. Someday soon, he reasoned, Preston would respond to all of this information on his own. Napping usually followed the long periods of reading, and at the end of the day, the Hammonds would reunite in Preston's room to gather around a laptop and read aloud the entries submitted that day to CaringBridge. The sincere words of encouragement from friends and family prompted reminiscences that took them far away from the medical statistics that saturated their minds. By late night, Brandon, Camille, and Krista would return to their designated sleeping spots in the waiting area, and Brian would settle into the recliner chair, where he routinely awakened each morning to the familiar sounds of the ventilator.

Typical mornings in acute care became defined by the commotion of staff during shift changes in the early hours. Upon awakening, Brian would strike up conversations with the nurses assigned to Preston's care that particular day. Learning more about their personal lives, helped him cope with his solemn surroundings. Sometimes he would inquire about the skiing conditions on the mountain, or ask a nurse or staff member about hobbies and interests outside of their work. Through his interactions with medical staff, he learned, first-hand, about prospective medical milestone plans for Preston, and more about some of the setbacks he was experiencing. The medical professionals also learned a great deal about my uncle. His dedication to his son and his family was evident as he remained vigilant about interacting with Preston's care. The rules may have bended a bit, by allowing a critical care patient's immediate family member to remain so close to a patient. But as the hours moved forward, staff depended on my uncle to assist with tasks that seemed tedious, but gratifying to my uncle. He would occasionally break for a cafeteria coffee run, or to grab a bite to eat or a quick morning shower at Krista and Preston's house, but always quickly returned to his bedside vigil next to his junior outdoorsman.

Although they valued Brian's dedication to remaining bedside to Preston, Camille and Krista and Brandon found it extremely difficult to remain in the quietness of his room hour after hour. Instead, they rotated their visits with Brian and Preston and spent shorter intervals next to him during the day, gathering around him for prayer and reflection during the evening hours. Their time was better spent during the day, they agreed, taking turns caring for Jackson and circulating among the continual stream of visitors who rotated in the waiting area. Talking to others now seemed to be the key to relieving some of the anxiety they were feeling in the quiet room, where moments were guided into hours by the humming and beeping sounds of the machines that delivered little encouragement.

Brian, on the other hand, rarely revealed himself to visitors. He was determined to remain close at hand, constantly watching the machines and monitors keeping Preston alive. For short intervals some afternoons, he would take a break and spend a few moments glancing out a window in a neighboring hallway. Often, the gray skies mirrored his spirit, but he tried not to let it show. Those afternoons were tough, but it was in the oncoming darkness of the long winter evenings at the end of the day, when the hallways and waiting areas were quiet, that Brian found it hardest to remain hopeful. I sensed that the hours of quiet and the fear of Preston's unknown outcome were gradually chipping away at my uncle's spirit. His weight was dropping, and his character seemed increasingly tattered and broken. It was not like anything I'd ever seen during my many visits to my aunt and uncle's house over the years. The recent weeks had stolen something from him. He wasn't the same rugged, confident man I grew up knowing. And I wondered if he had given up hope of regaining his son.

CHAPTER 10

I *remember meeting him for the first time when I was just nine years old. I was at that impressionable age and I watched the actions of those around me, carefully. Luckily for me, my aunt Camille didn't mind having me hang around occasionally, and I don't think she knew she fully understood how much I'd looked up to her as my role-model. On that particular day I was a passenger, she-the driver, in Mim and Pip's LTD. It was a gold "road boat" that, from my perspective, felt like it took up both sides of the road. And when Aunt Camille was behind the wheel, its broadness seemed glamorous, like I imagined we both were. That car traveled umpteen times around the entire radius of our tiny little safe haven of Page, Arizona, on afternoons when Camille would pick me up for a ride after school. I was happy to go anywhere in that car, as long as she was driving.*

On this particular day, she was enlightening me about how "good-looking" her new boyfriend was as she adjusted the radio dial to add crispness to one of the Carpenter's hit singles and maneuvered the LTD behind the Pink Sands ice cream shop on Main Street. Just as on previous outings, we used the drive-through window to grab sundaes before gliding into the parking area at the back of the shop to devour our treats. The tires smashed the black rubber hose, prompting the high-school girl at the drive-up window to take our order. We both asked for Camille's favorite—a caramel pineapple sundae, her own invention, which she assured me I would love- so I did. And then we would continue our rounds around town, stopping to talk about high-school things with some of her networks as I watched on, wishing I could hurry and grow up fast enough to fit in with her group of friends.

One day after circling the town listening to music, Camille and I went through the usual motions of the drive-through window, then directly to the parking lot behind the Pepto-Bismol–colored ice cream shop. And there he appeared, the new boyfriend—the one who would become my uncle. He had shoulder-length light-brown hair, a thick mustache, blue-jean over- alls, and he was wearing flip-flops. He was missing the shirt underneath the overalls, and only one of the straps of the overalls was attached. The other dangled across his broad, sun-tanned back. "Do you think he's cute?" Aunt Camille asked as he made his way to the driver's-side window. I nod- ded as I dragged my pink plastic spoon across the caramel sauce on my sundae.

Many after school trips to the ice cream shop and a few years later, wed- ding bells rang just a couple of miles down the road. On March 20, 1976, Camille Louise Fountain married that boy in the overalls, Brian Leon Hammond, in a late-afternoon ceremony at the Immaculate Heart of Mary Catholic Church in Page, Arizona. My younger sister and I were junior bridesmaids, and stood beneath the shadows of the floppy straw hats of the "real" bridesmaids. I had no real wedding responsibilities that day, but my status, junior bridesmaid, earned me a front-row seat at the ceremony. Aunt Camille made me feel appreciated by including me in the festivities of her wedding day. I felt special whenever she incorporated me into her plans and her wedding day was outstanding for me. On that spring day in March, wearing my special-occasion long dress and with my curls coated in hairspray, I watched her take on the new role of beautiful young wife, secretly hoping she would never forget how important it was for her to con- tinue to be my special aunt.

After the long-Catholic wedding mass and ceremony, we all dined on Polynesian fare, compliments of Mim's church-lady friend, who was a fabulous cook. We were all together that afternoon and evening as a family, laughing, eating and dancing. For me, that was the most comforting place to be in the world. As far as I was concerned, nothing terrible had ever happened to us. Through my childish eyes, nothing terrible had ever happened to the world, either. For me, life was in perfect alignment.

Our small town gained a married couple that day, while other couples and families, including mine, were dropping from its population due to the completion of the power plant construction project. In fact, the very next day, as the newlyweds flew off to Mexico for their honeymoon, my parents, my sister, and I followed the contents of our home in a moving van, out of the tiny little town that had become my safety net. We were relocating a couple of hours south to Flagstaff. We were all so busy with my aunt's wedding plans, I didn't have time to stress any occurrences beyond the day of their nuptials. But as we pulled away from my safety net our spot on the planet, I cried more tears than I'd ever remembered crying before. I was afraid of change—something that has forever followed me. More important, I was afraid of losing a connection with my aunt Camille.

One year after their wedding, on April 21, Camille gave birth to their first son, Preston Lee Hammond. Four years later, on July 10, his little brother, Brandon Daniel Hammond, was born.

CHAPTER 11

J ust five days after the accident, Preston was receiving dialysis
from a machine as a result of failing kidneys, and his every
breath continued to be assisted by a ventilator. Was the thriving
life he'd known just over a week ago forever lost? Had his fate been
decided by this terrible, unintended injury? Each day became a
roller-coaster—medically, and emotionally for everyone close to
my cousin.

Camille felt elated the day the kidney dialysis machine arrived
at Flagstaff Medical Center. Preston would be the first patient to
utilize it, and he desperately needed its support. The machine was
a new addition to the recently advanced trauma level care assigned
to the intensive care unit, and its arrival was a factor in keeping
Preston from being flown to a Phoenix hospital when he was initially stabilized. Camille and Brian felt completely confident about
the care Preston was receiving under Dr. Donnelly's orders at
FMC, thus the filtering process was set to begin. Brian assisted
nurses and technicians with the setup of the machine that would
filter Preston's blood of excess water and waste products, because
his own kidneys were no longer doing the job. My aunt watched as
Brian read the instructions to staff members during the meticulous

assembly of the machine. His involvement with Preston's care never wavered, and was a sign of reassurance to Camille that, despite his physical exhaustion, he was still mentally intact.

By December 6, there was a spark of hope stemming from a tiny achievement. For the first time, Preston's ventilator would be turned down for small intervals of time to test his ability to breathe on his own. There were small steps like this that offered extremely slight bits of progress. Every process was one step forward, and many times two steps back.

As the days at the hospital progressed, every small, fulfilling milestone was praised, and every setback was grieved. Whether it was the amount of Preston's urine output or an eye flutter as the result of a command, the baby steps forward were celebrated as great events by doctors, nurses, and his family. For the first time since the accident, Preston's wife, Krista, told me that she felt encouraged by Preston's struggle to open his eyes to see her. She sensed that he knew of her presence in the room, despite his comatose state. It was these fragments of encouragement that we all clung to during the first few days and weeks.

But the enjoyment from the initial breakthrough of ventilator weaning was short-lived. By December 8, a whole new set of medical complications occurred. Adding to the sting of severely failing kidneys and rhabdomyolysis (death of muscle fibers due to injury), Preston developed a lung infection, which quickly turned into pneumonia. He would have to be returned to the operating table for placement of a jugular catheter and a tracheostomy, and undergo a procedure to flush his lungs. Immediate concerns about his ability to withstand a second operation took over the Hammond's thoughts. Dr. Donnelly was vigilant as he explained to them that the additional surgical procedures *weren't* optional.

Following his second surgery, Preston appeared to be resting comfortably, although seemed almost lifeless again. There were no tiny eye flutters to get excited over, and his heavy sedation seemed to remove some of the progress of those little reactions he had recently communicated. It was hard for his family to accept what seemed like a regression in his condition. Dr. Donnelly instructed them that the possibility of his recovery could now be determined day by day. This was an improvement from his previous hour-to-hour prognosis. The doctor's words conveyed little hope, and still didn't sound optimistic.

Brandon and Camille met with Dr. Donnelly later that evening, during his rounds. His report left little to be celebrated. Carefully spoken words were impossible for them to forget. "Frankly, I am surprised that Preston is alive," the doctor said. "In my medical career, I have never seen anyone survive the obstacles Preston has thus far survived: one, kidney failure; two, heart failure; and three, the amount of blood loss."

In conversations among family members in the hallway near the waiting room, we had learned shortly after Preston's initial surgery that he'd lost an extensive amount of blood before he even entered the emergency room. The massive blood loss alone was enough to cause death or, more than likely, severe mental issues. During the operation to save him, he'd received eighteen units of packed cells, seventeen units of fresh-frozen plasma, sixteen units of platelets, and two units of cryoprecipitate. In medical terms, those amounts didn't mean a lot to us. But common sense told us he'd lost way too much. Because Preston had lost more than five of his twelve pints of blood, he was destined to enter into a state of hypovolemic shock, which he did. And the massive blood loss most likely meant mental, tissue, and organ damage. This was exactly the medical path Preston was taking.

The floor beneath their feet became the focal point, and again Dr. Donnelly determined that Preston's life would be measured day by day, and the probability of brain damage due to the amount of blood loss was high—if he survived at all.

The entries on CaringBridge poured in that day.

Dear Camille,

I couldn't sleep. My heart is aching for you and your family. I know it's been a hard couple of days. A dear friend told me once, "A mother's prayers are always answered." You and your family have a lot of loved ones sending love and prayers your way. I feel in my heart Preston will make it through this. Could you give Brandon a hug for me? Tell him we love him too. Brian too.

Louise

Another, from James:

I wish you a speedy and full recovery. You are constantly in my thoughts. We go back a long way, my friend. I remember us playing ball at Children's Park for endless days as kids. It is awesome that we both had the chance to play some hard ball this past summer. I think you went two for two or three for three during that game. And, you made that sliding catch in right field, even though you were playing out of position—you're an infielder! Very impressive for not swinging a bat in years.

You have an impact on many people, it's obvious to see in the journal entries.

When you get back on your feet let's go fishing?

Often, when I returned to visit my cousin at the medical center on weekends, I would find Aunt Camille, Uncle Brian, Brandon, Krista, and little Jackson arranged in the same places in the hospital that I had seen them the week before. It was as if time stood still for them. I wondered how they would escape this horrible situation and with what outcome would they leave the hospital. I could completely sympathize with Krista. She talked about trying to visualize a hopeful future, and told me she wanted nothing more than to return to the life she knew as a newlywed and a new mother. I tried to comfort her, assuring her that her feelings were normal and valid and that I understood how taxing it must have been to keep her energy and optimism divided between Jackson's needs and supporting her husband through his critical state.

In reality, I'm not sure I understood the impact of what she was going through at all. I'd never experienced anything like it before. I knew she hadn't given up on him, but it was evident she had doubts that Preston would return home, and I wasn't sure anything I could say would change how she felt. I wondered what, if anything, Preston might be experiencing mentally in his state of altered consciousness. Was he communicating with his Savior? Were decisions being made about him staying in this world or moving forward to his life in eternity? Did he see segments of his life being replayed, or was his mind completely at rest as it worked to help him heal himself inside? I craved to know more about his journey, and hoped I'd be given the opportunity to talk to him about his experience. The most outstanding of all of my observations during my visits at the hospital was the essence of patience evident among the Hammonds, who never once wavered from their faith.

I'm not sure which was harder, knowing Preston was struggling for survival or watching his family suffer through the process. I questioned how the Hammonds could continue to remain strong each day, when most days seemed rather hopeless. *Will God answer their prayers?* I wondered. Or would it be the odds of nature that would determine my cousin's outcome following this tragedy? Was the power of prayer coming through from the numbers of those banded together in hope of his recovery? Or was God listening solely to Aunt Camille and Uncle Brian, specifically because they remained focused and faithful to Him? My guilt over abandoning faith in recent months made me feel shameful. So, I continued to watch as an outsider silently, hoping God would show me that He was listening to the prayers being poured out by all of us on my cousin Preston's behalf.

When I reflected on Preston's life on those visiting weekends, it seemed as if his growing-up years had sprinted by like a race. Now more than ever, I needed more time, more memories with my cousin—we all did. Was it too much to ask for more life for him?

Preston Lee Hammond was born on April 21, 1977. I was thirteen years old and returned to Page, from Flagstaff, to attend his first birthday party. It was a living-room, coffee-table celebration with just a few attendees. We sang and clapped our hands as Preston blew out the single candle that sat proudly on top of the homemade double-layer cake frosted with Mim's simple shortening, butter, and powdered-sugar recipe. That modest festivity fed my dreaming young teenage spirit as I observed Aunt Camille's enthusiasm as a new mom.

Preston eventually had to share special occasions with his new younger brother, Brandon. Birthday celebrations and their youthful years seemed to pass quickly, and I visited often to watch them unfold.

I'm not sure how the next years got away so quickly, but I know I enjoyed a dozen or more Lake Powell boating trips with my aunt, uncle and young cousins while growing up. The memories of outings on the lake where the wind whipped through our hair, peeling it away from our sunburned faces as the boat's bow slapped the greenish-blue waves are forever planted in my mind. I recall the occasional search to find the perfect beach, and my young cousins jumping into the lake, from the boats bow, to cool off. I remember hot afternoons sunbathing in lawn chairs with our feet dangling into the water as we raced through the pages of fashion magazines, in search of next season's perfect swimsuit. And I cannot forget my uncle letting me drive his convertible around their neighborhood until the gasoline ran out, when I turned 16. With every visit, an outdoor activity of some sort was planned, and that kept me coming back for more each and every year; it still does.

Along with the visits to her house, I loved Aunt Camille's energy and the way she always arranged those stays with interactive fun. Throughout my teen years, there was comfort in returning to the small town that I'd once called home—the same town where Camille graduated from high school and met and married Brian, where I took my first swimming lessons as a youngster and walked to elementary school. It was the place where I sat in the front row at her wedding ceremony, and where my admiration for my aunt had begun as she'd transformed from high-school cheerleader to girl-friend to wife and mother. My feeling of wonder for her continued as she raised two young boys through the eighties and nineties, until eventually my cousins became confident outdoorsmen.

CHAPTER 12

For a string of painfully long days, only a few medically insignificant advances in the recovery process took place in acute care for Preston. But now, even the superficial improvements were proving to be as vital as the medical ones for his family. Even the simplest steps forward in the regaining process were celebrated each day. One day was highlighted by the simplicity of a clean shave, compliments of one of my cousin's nurses. Shortly after being cleaned up, Preston received a kiss from my uncle Brian, and about three seconds following that kiss, Preston reacted by puckering his lips at the loving gesture from his dad. This kind of advancement, although small, produced sighs of relief and praise among us. It was the kind of encouragement the family needed to get through this process.

As I continued to watch them express satisfaction over the minor accomplishments, I began to realize the positive impact their support was having on Preston and each other. The celebrations of small victories kept each of them encouraging the others, reaching forward for more positive developments, breaking barriers that had seemed impossible before. And even if everything wasn't working as it should have been on his insides, my cousin was beginning to supply physical signals, with eye flutters and finger movements, indicating that he understood what was going on in the world around him.

The bullet that had pierced Preston's wrist and chest had somehow refrained from fragmenting or mushrooming on impact. How that happened remained a mystery to all of us. It even caused the medical team to shake their heads in disbelief. We were thankful the statistics hadn't prevailed. Days after the accident, I had heard possible scenarios tossed around the waiting room, none with positive outcomes. I tried to shield myself from one particular conversation. I didn't want to hear it, but knew it was true. "Because the chest cavity houses the central nervous system and the cardiac and pulmonary anatomy, it was the worst possible place anyone could ever take a bullet," whispered a member of the medical staff, standing among a small group of our extended family. The fact was, in most scenarios, statistically, if the destruction from the bullet wound to the chest doesn't kill the victim, infection most likely will. Those statistics were frightening. But there we sat, continuing to ponder the mystery of it all. As the clock ticked on, life somehow sustained itself within my cousin.

As traces of snow fell silently outside the windows of the medical center during the slow-moving month of December, a team of dedicated doctors, nurses, and medical specialists continued to do all they could to help my cousin survive. The smallest developmental progress remained encouraging enough to nourish the Hammonds' spirits and help them maintain control over their anxiety during the grueling process of reclamation as they continually prayed for a return to normal life for my cousin—for all of them. With each passing day, the Hammonds held themselves and each other together through the negative and positive updates with the assistance of their unwavering faith and the giant outpouring of support from extended family and friends. Sometimes the pauses between guest visits caused the hallways at the medical center to become eerie and quiet. It was during those times when the sound of the ventilator pumping oxygen and the hum of the kidney dialysis machine became too familiar.

Preston's friend Megan hadn't seen him since they attended after-school religious classes at the Immaculate Heart of Mary church, but she heard about his accident through a friend of a friend she remained connected to in Page. She wrote the following inspiring message to him and his family on CaringBridge, which had already received more than 2,000 entries. It was exactly the inspiration the Hammonds needed that evening:

Preston and Family,

I was reading this morning and thinking of you all. Proverbs says "this too shall pass," which is something my dad used to tell me growing up. It is true. It seems that you are doing a little better each day—keep up the fight and stay strong.

My mom has these candles that you gave her from CCD classes. I can remember hearing my mom say, "Preston Hammond gave these to me." It's funny, but I've never forgotten that. And I've never been able to find anything like them, or you. Stay strong.

Megan

Aunt Camille, normally full of hope and happiness, had become much more focused on her family's immediate needs and quieter over the passing weeks, as if following a path that could only be taken with precise steps on her own personal journey, through her own faith. She found comfort in writing her personal reflections during the quiet afternoons, journaling daily events, visitors' comments, and medical information in a small, weathered journal titled *Footprints*, given to her by a visiting friend. Her friend, Tammy, wrote a personal message on the inside cover of the first page. In the message, she apologized for the condition of the worn outside cover of the journal, and noted that she was touched by the words of encouragement printed on the cover and throughout its pages. Her attractive script handwriting encouraged my aunt to focus on the inside of the book, and herself.

The condition of the journal harmonized with Preston's physical condition—tattered on the outside, complex on the inside. The gift was meant to be merely a "guest book" that Camille could later reflect upon. It surely would serve as a great recollection of those who came to show their support during an extremely difficult time. The valued journal was small enough for Camille to tuck into her purse, but large enough to fill with notes of progression and visitors' names on its lined pages. It was the color of a warm autumn sunset, and the cover depicted a sandy beach alongside a serene ocean at low tide, the tranquil sand marked with a single set of footprints. A familiar poem of promise, whose author is unknown, was printed on the inside cover and served as a continual reminder that the Hammonds were being carried through this serious disruption in their lives and their prayers were being heard throughout this process of unknowns.

Footprints
One night a man had a dream.
He dreamed he was walking along the beach with the Lord.
Across the dark sky flashed scenes from his life.
For each scene, he noticed two sets of footprints in the sand,
One belonging to him and the other to the Lord.
When the last scene of his life flashed before him,
He looked back at the footprints in the sand.
He noticed that at many times along the path of his life
There was only one set of footprints. He also noticed that it
Happened at the very lowest and saddest times of his life.

This really bothered him and he questioned the Lord about it.
"Lord, you said that once I decided to follow you,
You'd walk with me all the way.
But I noticed that during the most troublesome times of my life,
there is only one set of footprints.
I don't understand why, when I needed You the most, you would
   leave me.
The Lord replied "My precious child, I love you and will never
   leave you!
During your times of trial and suffering
When you see only one set of footprints,
It was then that I carried you."

The journal became a cherished record, offering meaning and solace that winter. It turned out to be much more than just a guest book. It's funny how something small like that can become so important in someone's emotional recovery process. Camille hoped she could look back on it in the future as a reminder of the wonderful people and positive medical advances that pulled her son through the most dreadful accident imaginable. The empty lined pages slowly became filled with thoughts and pictures and prayers.

Yet despite the distraction of journaling, the reality of Preston's condition kept tapping on her shoulder each day like an unwelcome nightmare, and those fears were also reflected in her words. But the routine of taking time to include daily entries and the ability to flip the pages back to notations of encouraging progress helped keep her focused-on optimism during the seemingly endless days and nights at her unintended temporary home, the waiting area of the intensive care unit. Many of her journal entries marked the frustrations of days that revealed little or no medical improvement, while others reflected optimism in the long recovery road yet to be traveled. They are reflected upon today with recollections of mysterious happenings that have a valued meaning that she was unable to appreciate when she wrote them down.

One of the entries described the trouble that the medical staff had with the kidney dialysis machine and how its malfunction made her fear it might stop working altogether. Another was an account of improvement in Preston's breathing, as the ventilator was once again lowered. One day was accounted for in a single number—simply the scribbled balance of the Wells Fargo assistance account opened by our cousin Hollie, in Preston's name. That total served as an encouraging reminder to my aunt that the outside world was not giving up on a sometimes seemingly hopeless situation. Many pages of the memoir were filled with the names of people who visited and the gifts they brought. Some of the names were of strangers, until that winter. They belonged to people visiting other patients whose lives had also been placed on hold by ill-fated situations. Tiny crosses were added in front of their names, one for each time Camille prayed for them in the hospital chapel.

A single lengthy account within a number of tea-stained pages highlighted by scripture described the empathy Camille felt for the families entering the emergency room doors every day and night. Her accounts detailed the agony she felt when she saw the tears and the distressed looks on the faces of those just beginning to encounter an unknown medical future as her family was. She recounted the sounds of families sobbing as they huddled with loved ones and how those cries had become too commonly heard. And she wrote about the common threads of emotion between her family and the other grieving families, despite the vast differences in medical conditions. Some were there as a result of car accidents, others overdoses, and some grave illnesses. Every family had the common thread of an unknown future.

When she wasn't writing or reflecting, Camille would sometimes sit at Preston's bedside with Brian. Occasionally the two of them would walk through the hallways of the hospital—catching up with each other, making sure the other was doing okay emotionally—and make a plan for how they would get beyond the next twenty-four hours, come what may. They would recount the progress of each day, clarifying the numbers on the life-saving machines and encourage each other to continue to be strong. They would ask each other if they were interpreting the doctors' notes in the same way, and they would confirm a watchful eye on Brandon, making sure one or the other was offering him reassurance. Sometimes the two of them would talk with other families in the hallways of the emergency waiting areas. As grieving parents, they would offer their support to other families and seek some for themselves too. It was small social intervals like this that kept them rational.

Day after day, the long hours of uncertainty and mental stress of Preston's unknown future continued to march on. Months after the accident, Camille told me that she was unable to spend long periods of time in Preston's hospital room because of overwhelming anxiety and fear. She remembered how it disturbed her to watch the all-too-familiar routine of undertakers appearing late at night through a side entrance by the waiting area to retrieve the bodies of those who had surrendered in their fight for life behind the cold steel of the emergency-room doors. She couldn't keep her composure when the figures covered in white cloth were rolled down a darkened hallway and greeted by the freezing night outside those doors.

To pass the somber, slow-moving time one evening, Camille journaled about her conversation the previous night with a beautiful slender black woman whom she believed to be about her age. She noted that the fluorescent lighting near the nurse's station, where she nearly bumped into her, was especially kind to her dark, smooth complexion, pointing out the fact that it radiated clarity, as did her saucer-shaped chocolate brown eyes. The well-dressed woman seemed extremely calmly composed, and my aunt initially mistook her for a member of the medical staff. It wasn't until the woman told Camille why she was there that the conversation shifted.

The woman explained that she was the mother of a critical car-accident patient. She was pacing the tile floors near the nurse's station as she waited for her son to come out of surgery. It then seemed strange to my aunt that the woman had no family members accompanying her for support in the waiting room. Camille felt especially connected to this woman, who talked calmly and waited alone for the outcome of her son's situation. Hours earlier, she told my aunt, his mangled body had been extracted from a crumpled car on the interstate. He had been rushed through the same cold steel doors behind which Preston had disappeared days earlier, she explained. The attractive woman and my aunt exchanged details about their children's accidents for a long time that evening, both expressing gratitude for the good fortune of their lives intersecting in the intensive care unit. As they talked, beneath a clock that seemingly wasn't moving, the woman asked at one point if she could hug my aunt. While embracing Camille, she whispered softly into her ear, "Your son is going to make it. I feel the presence of God here."

Layered between the sounds of the overhead pager and the continuous movement of emergency medical staff, the two continued to exchange sentiments of appreciation for each other's company for an extended length of time. Finally, Camille said her temporary good-byes, promising to resume their discussion after obtaining Dr. Donnelly's daily report. Camille made her way toward the nurse's station to compare Preston's vitals with the previous day's, and scour staff notes for any anticipated tidbits of progress for the day. When she returned to the waiting area to share the details of her findings, the woman was gone, never returning to that waiting area again. Camille was unable to obtain any information about the woman's whereabouts, nor did she ever learn the outcome of her son's medical circumstances—hospital policy, she assumed.

Had he survived? What about the surgery? Would the young man be transferred to a room near Preston's? Several mornings later, after walking the hallways of intensive care and peering through the alternative places she thought she might find her new acquaintance, she wrote in her journal that it bothered her to think of things not turning out well.

CHAPTER 13

By the ninth day of December, signs of Christmas were popping up everywhere. Streetlight poles were being embellished outside the hospital's entrance, twinkling lights appeared in potted plants near the lobby, and teams of nurses were competing for votes in a gingerbread house contest, set up near one of their stations in acute care. Even though each of us wanted the world to pause and wait for my cousin to recover, time refused to stand still and kept moving closer and closer to the Christmas holiday. Without a doubt, this one would be different from any other for the Hammonds.

Back at the west-side Home Depot store, the busy holiday season meant that abundant supplies of fresh spruce, pine, juniper, and Douglas fir trees were being delivered to Flagstaff stores from an Oregon farm. Every year, Preston had been in charge of seeing that those deliveries were received on time and arranged properly, by characteristics of height and kind, within the temporary fenced lot just outside the garden center doors. This year, one of the store's assistant managers, Janelle, was filling in to make sure that all holiday shipments were processed and displayed as usual. Preston would have done the same, had he not been derailed.

As with most retail stores, the holiday season was a particularly prosperous time of year for Home Depot and a time when corporate looked at the sales numbers closely. Janelle understood the importance of the significant rise in those numbers and how each of the local stores competed for maximum dollars. She knew the demands of selling the products and the rise in stress that came with the pressures of this selling season. Determined to uphold Preston's outstanding sales numbers, Janelle worked particularly hard that December to make him proud.

The enthusiasm of Christmas usually radiated throughout the store with the background of seasonal music, but this year was different. Some of the ambition was missing at the store. Underneath their cherry-red Santa hats, employees were fulfilling their job duties in a somewhat somber manner. And discussions about Preston's grave condition were an ongoing topic in the break room. Some employees shook their heads sympathetically and others agreed that my cousin's situation overshadowed the usual enjoyment of the season at work. Despite the ambience that the sleigh bells and the smell of evergreens were supposed to provide, the atmosphere at the west-side store felt gloomy, especially to Janelle.

Preston had hired Janelle, who was bubbly and heartwarmingly enthusiastic, several years earlier to work in the paint department at the west-side store. She was exactly what he looked for in an employee—smart, meticulously groomed, reliable, and creative. Her noteworthy work ethic and desire to learn were the traits that helped her quickly climb up the ranks to assistant store manager just a couple of years after joining the associates team at Home Depot. Preston could count on Janelle to meet a deadline or produce a missing-link solution to an unsolved management situation. Now, she was here for him again, filling in extra shifts on his behalf and visiting his family routinely at the hospital.

Within a week following the accident, Janelle was working diligently with Home Depot's corporate office and the Red Cross to coordinate and host a blood drive at the store on Preston's behalf. The drive would be another way that she could make a positive difference despite his current unfortunate situation. Working behind the scenes after her shifts on the sales floor, Janelle contacted corporate and arranged for permission to utilize the west-side location for blood collection. Soon, she was assisting in transforming the break room into a three-station donation area.

Employees, family members, customers, and people from the community were among those who came through the doors to donate on the opening day of the drive. Donors made their way through Home Depot's conference room, which functioned as a screening area, before advancing to the makeshift contribution area. Meanwhile, back in Preston's hometown of Page, a second blood drive was taking place in his name, again with tremendous success. Within a couple of hours, forty units of blood were collected, completely replenishing the bank with the amount that Preston had required after the accident. It was another triumph that deserved to be celebrated.

One evening after completing her shift at the store, Janelle stopped by the hospital, like she did most evenings, for a short visit with Preston's family. Tonight, her purpose was to deliver gift cards purchased by Preston's coworkers for the Hammond family. She also wanted to share the good news about the success of the blood drive. Still running on the adrenaline of those preparations, Janelle rolled into a parking spot near the front doors of the medical center. She stomped her feet, releasing the ice from her boots, and peeled the hood from her buttoned coat to make her way through the large glass doors. That night, she felt warmhearted about the support of the community, and also because of the obvious signs of Christmas that she saw at the medical center. For the first time since the accident, she felt the wheels of progress turning in the right direction with the help of the community. Bristlecone garland embellished with miniature candy canes and greeting cards lined the counter at the coffee station in the front lobby of the hospital. Fresh poinsettia plants filled the atrium just outside the cafeteria, making the hospital feel alive again—unlike the way it had felt in recent weeks.

The holiday had been mostly forgotten by the Hammonds, who had set up a makeshift camp in the acute-care unit. While making her way through the hallways, it occurred to Janelle that it might be a thoughtful gesture to bring some kind of small gift of her own for the Hammonds. *A cross might be nice,* she thought as she passed the gift shop. A quick U-turn, and she was purchasing a cross-shaped wooden tree ornament. And as she dug into her wallet for the correct change, she felt a tiny bit frustrated that Home Depot's corporate policy was strict about selling only nonreligious seasonal items in all of its stores. This year, for the first time, that policy annoyed her more than ever before.

After grabbing her receipt and finishing up some small talk with the cashier about the frigid outdoor temperatures, Janelle wound through the decked hallways and back to the emergency wing. A pinecone wreath accented with a deep-green satin ribbon hung on an otherwise bland wall above the nurse's station just down the hall from Preston's colorless room. That was Janelle's destination each time she visited. She was sure to connect with a family member there among the medical staff. That evening, she met Krista pacing up and down the hallway. After handing her the gifts and opening her arms for a hug, Janelle inquired about Preston again.

Although she couldn't bring herself to see Preston personally while he was lying in a coma, looking so unlike himself, she made it a point to visit frequently with Krista, Camille, Brian, or Brandon in the hallways. She usually brought encouraging messages and get-well cards from employees at the store, and she also collected updates from the Hammonds on Preston's condition to share with coworkers the following day at work. This evening, she planned to share her news about the successful blood drive. But her enthusiasm about the drive was banished even before she began. It was evident that Krista had been struggling with emotion tonight. "It wouldn't and shouldn't have happened," she told Janelle, "if only he'd *not* gone out hunting that day. I know it doesn't seem important now, but the Christmas lights…if he'd just stayed home."

Understanding Krista's frustration from the long hours and days she'd been spending at Preston's bedside, Janelle held back her report about the blood drive and comforted Krista, fighting back her own tears. What should have been a season of joy and celebration for the recently married mother of a two-year-old had turned into weeks of tears and sadness. It was difficult to see Krista in her current situation—watching and waiting as the complications of her husband's condition multiplied.

After spending an emotional evening with Krista, Janelle mentioned that the employees at the store were getting together the very next evening for the annual Christmas party—an event Krista had completely forgotten about in recent weeks. Janelle said that it would be uplifting for the employees if someone from Preston's family attended the gathering to update the concerned coworkers and members of the management team about Preston's condition. Krista agreed to talk with her family, and said that one of them would stop by.

When Janelle returned home from the hospital that evening, she added words for reflection on CaringBridge, in hopes that Brian would read them to Preston that night before going to sleep. Her guest book entry was from a song she heard that night while driving home after her visit with Krista and Camille. The song, by Joe Nichols, is titled "The Impossible." Janelle found it fitting, considering the recent days of medical twists and turns for Preston and his family.

"Unsinkable ships sink, unbreakable walls break. Sometimes the things you think could never happen, happens just like that. Unbreakable steel bends, if the fury of the wind is unstoppable. I've learned to never underestimate the impossible."

Her concluding thoughts in the message spoke of never underestimating the huge support system or the power of love that surround Preston and his family during this trial. And with that wish for his family, Janelle cried herself to sleep.

The next day, the Hammonds decided that Uncle Brian would attend Home Depot's Christmas party briefly to give a synopsis of Preston's condition. They all agreed that Brian could use a break from the confines of the hospital room. And besides, he was the one best informed medically to talk to the group of concerned co-workers. But before the evening Christmas party started, the day-light hours unfolded terribly for him.

Earlier that day, Dr. Donnelly had delivered a blow to the family. It seemed like somehow, he could magically predict Preston's up-coming troubling days. He prepared the Hammonds with a medical forecast—and it was spot-on accurate. On Sunday, December 10, the same day that the Home Depot Christmas party was sched-uled, complications of pneumonia and liver function became huge setbacks in my cousin's progress. In addition, he had developed acute liver failure, which was extremely dangerous, presenting a whole new set of life-threatening complications. As Dr. Donnelly explained it, a liver that doesn't function properly can cause ex-cess fluid to build pressure in the brain, meaning that infection is more likely to set in and kidney failure is likely to follow. This would be an additional critical setback and would add to Preston's list of medical complications to overcome.

It was determined that pneumonia had settled into Preston's lungs due to his obvious lack of mobility and as a result of infected fluid building up within the layers of tissue between his lungs and his chest wall. The even more serious secondary hindrance was that infection had now spread to his liver. It was difficult to keep up with removing the excess fluid building within his brain. This dangerous turn of events could easily progress, causing his kidneys and then other organs to shut down completely.

The report left those surrounding Preston's bedside that morning with deflated spirits. Hours of silence blanketed his room, and for many long intervals, only the sounds of the humming machines around him could be heard. The Hammonds took a break from seeing visitors for the entire day and focused solely on prayer and comforting each other. Late that afternoon, Brian's voice broke the silence of the room as he stated that he would update Preston's coworkers at the party. He said it was something he *needed* to do.

He had no intention of being the guest of honor at the party his son should have been enjoying that evening. He could almost see Preston and Krista mingling among the party guests, raising appetizer plates to their chins, while Preston's recognizable laugh occasionally interrupted light conversation between him and his associates. He remembered how Preston anticipated the annual Christmas party each year; it was an opportunity to break away from the stress of management and the requirements from corporate. Instead, his son lay motionless, connected to machines that were keeping his failing organs from surrendering. Still, the words he would share with Preston's concerned coworkers needed to be heard. There was genuine concern among them, and they continued to seek ways to help his family.

Brian was the one who could pull himself together enough to speak in front of a crowd. He was the one who knew the details of the accident, and now the meaning of the numbers on the monitors that confirmed his son's unstable condition. As he drove away from the medical center, across town to the holiday gathering, he thought carefully about the amount of information he would reveal to the concerned group. He wasn't going to lose hope for recovery, and he didn't want anyone listening to the statistics to lose hope either. He thought carefully about the right things to say. He wasn't properly dressed for the occasion, he remembered, when he glanced down at his camouflage pants in the parking lot before entering the party. It would be okay, he assured himself. He'd spent the past two weeks wearing alternating sets of hunting gear in the intensive care unit with Preston. Until he went to speak at the party, he hadn't thought about the camos. That night, the pants were a firm reminder of the morning of the hunt.

Brian was warmly greeted at the party with embraces from several of Preston's closest coworkers. No one seemed to mind how he was dressed that evening. He surveyed the large dining area with its cloth-lined decorated tables. He noted the large potluck spread of food and those gathered around it, filling their plates. The aroma of the warm pots of comfort foods reminded him of the holiday that Preston was about to miss. He fixated on the podium with a microphone at the front of the room, where one of the store managers was reflecting on the past year's sales report from the east- and west-side stores. In the background he heard faint Christmas music. Later he remembered that the sound of the music comforted him a bit; it was a welcome contrast to the hum of Preston's life-support machines.

He was nervous, he recalled, and didn't fully know how to tell the large group gathered for the celebration that Preston might never return home or to his job again. But at that point, he remembered, his only wish was that he would somehow maintain life. As he was introduced and continued toward the front of the room, he scraped together his courage and fought back tears as he spoke just long enough to thank everyone for their outpouring of concern and love. He mentioned that it was comforting to see all of the familiar faces that evening and thanked the group, whose eyes seem to connect directly with his in sympathy. He concluded that he was unable to offer much hope for a bright outcome for Preston that night, noting that his progress had become quite turbulent over the last twenty-four hours. He abruptly bowed his head and ended his summary of Preston's condition and slipped through the door. He returned to Preston's bedside, watching the machines all through the night as they continued to pump life into his son's struggling body.

Sometime during that evening, the following words of encouragement to Preston appeared on CaringBridge, which his dad read to him before going to sleep that night:

Preston, this is our prayer for you, that your light shall break forth like the morning, and your healing, your restoration and the power of a new life will spring forth speedily. (Isaiah 58:8) May God bless and keep you and your family,

Steve, Misty, Cidney and Lindsey

CHAPTER 14

The next morning, doctors drained a liter of fluid from Preston's chest cavity. Failing organs coupled with the large amounts of fluid doctors were administering and the weeks of ventilation were keeping Preston's system from excreting fluids properly. He was swollen to the point of being almost unrecognizable. His body weight had climbed in recent days from his normal 165 pounds to more than 250 pounds. After the drainage procedure, he was weak and agitated, so heavy sedation was again required. That meant another day of no interaction with family and visitors.

The medically induced slumber kept Preston from comprehending any of the conversation with Gary, his past store manager, who had stopped by the hospital in hopes of seeing Preston and visiting with his family the morning following the Christmas celebration. Gary had been transferred to a store in southern Arizona several months prior. He was talking to Camille in the hallway across from Preston's room, recalling the previous night's party. He added gratitude for Brian's ability to step in front of the crowd to deliver a courageous update on Preston's condition. He told my aunt about the postparty gathering in Preston and Krista's front yard.

It was Janelle's idea to festively decorate the exterior of their house, knowing how much it would mean to Krista and little Jackson. As he explained it, a group of employees gathered after the evening's festivities and returned briefly to the west-side store to gather a few ladders, boxes of colored light strands, extension cords, and light-up inflatable holiday figures, including a Santa and reindeer set for Jackson, and a polar bear holding a fishing pole, which would have been Preston's favorite. Camille and Gary chuckled a bit as Gary described the team of "elves" scurrying around the front yard, working together that freezing night, to brighten the Hammonds' spirits. He added that Jackson peeked from a window in the front of the house. His face, illuminated by the outdoor lights, looked adorable as he watched the activity and was a sight, Gary said, he wouldn't soon forget.

Afterwards, his lightheartedness gave way to a quieter, more serious tone, and he mentioned the angel, as if he doubted Camille would believe him, and doubted he'd really seen her himself.

It's unclear who had spotted her first—most likely, it was Gabe, who worked in electrical. And credit for the initial sighting was never a topic for debate. In fact, no one ever took credit for placing her up there; doing so would have certainly drawn reprimand from corporate due to the (unlikely) possibility that she would fall and hurt someone. Besides, who would have gone to the trouble of securing anything that high in the rafters, and when would he or she have done it? The task would have been tough, even with the assistance of an order picker. Why hadn't anyone mentioned it to the Hammonds yet? It wasn't important. What was important, though, was her existence in the store and the universal knowledge of her presence among employees.

The angel had first been spotted two days after the accident, and the news had spread like wildfire through all the departments. She was situated approximately twenty-five feet up in the rafters above the wire-cutting machine, where she was illuminated day and night by the lamps and chandeliers beneath her in the electrical department. Employees described her as a lifelike Christmas-tree topper with beautiful features. She had an iridescent face, with large blue eyes and dainty red lips. Her flowing white dress had movement to it, mostly due to the airflow from heat vents in the ceiling. Her shimmering wings moved slightly like a butterfly's, and were mostly visible from the store aisles when the light from the chandeliers caught them.

For almost a year following Preston's accident, she floated there, where she seemed to be looking down on the store activity beneath her. Employees pointed fingers at who among them might have dared to secure her there, but no one ever fessed up. Many of the employees purposefully visited that department during their shifts, to glance up and make sure she was still there—the spiritual attendant that coworkers universally referred to as "Preston's angel." No one pointed her out to customers, and customers didn't seem to know she was there at all. It is rumored that the angel was removed the winter following Preston's accident, but by whom? Her whereabouts are unknown. Her existence was a topic of conversation among employees at the west-side store for a number of years following her visit and the coincidence of her presence ties directly to the Hammond's beliefs about celestial beings watching over us from above. Surely her presence had impacted Gary, or he never would have mentioned it to Camille. Their conversation that day was uplifting, and learning about the gestures of friends and the occurrence of the angel gave my aunt a sense of peace that she desperately needed that day.

Questions about the uncertain medical prognosis remained the focus for most visitors for the next few days. By now, news about the accident had saturated the small town of Page. Family members from neighboring cities and states were united with the locals in their concern. It's as if we all had something to learn about this tragedy, this medical mystery, all of us pulling together in prayer.

Medical-center staff told the Hammonds that they had never seen that many supporters and visitors come through their hallways for one person. Joel, the Guardian Medical Transport driver who had brought Preston in from the Summit fire station on November 30, stopped by the waiting room occasionally to check on him and talk with my uncle Brian. The two of them exchanged their thoughts about Preston's grave condition each time. They were both equally astounded by the fact that the bullet had not done more internal damage.

Suffering. It's more than just unpleasant physical pain. It's also something that burdens the mind and emotions and interferes with the ability to feel. A considerable amount of suffering and fear was inundating my cousin and his family in recent weeks. The distressing sensation made some days uncomfortable and others unbearable. The fact that Preston was enduring such hardship was agonizing for everyone who loved him. I believed his condition caused each of us take a step back, however, in gratitude for our own health, and reminded us of the fragility of our own lives. Without a doubt, the odds were against him, but Preston wasn't letting odds determine his fate. The Hammonds' questions with each passing day were now the obvious ones. If he survived, would he have brain damage? Would he live for the rest of his life only with the help of machines, in a vegetative state, forever lacking awareness? Would he be paralyzed? How could he possibly be the same person they had known before the accident?

And suddenly there came a turning point.

CHAPTER 15

A couple of weeks after Janelle pulled together the successful blood drive, after the angel had appeared in the rafters at the west-side Home Depot store (and her presence prominently noted in Aunt Camille's journal), and the exhilaration had settled from the holiday brilliance of Krista and Preston's illuminated front yard, compliments of those generous coworkers, Preston's condition slowly began to improve.

By December 12, Dr. Donnelly's daily reports to the family finally had an air of encouragement. For the first time since the accident, Brandon heard more confidence in the tone of the doctor's voice. It finally hinted at optimism about his brother's recovery. For an entire week, Dr. Donnelly's medical updates turned the spirits of family members from fear and anxiety to joy and hope. Finally, his reports related with specific intention the slow but steady progress of Preston's organs, adding that he and his staff had openly agreed in recent morning briefings that Preston held within him "great healing power."

Brandon could feel his own heart pumping again, and the nightmare of his brother's medical struggles slowly subsiding. It was as if, he too, was awakening from an emotional sleep. He could now look Dr. Donnelly in the eye and completely trust the confidence in his words. He had privately gauged his brother's condition almost solely on Donnelly's tone and body language, often too numb to hear the actual words. But today was different. Today there was optimism. This was the turning point they had been waiting patiently for.

Each day, Preston's kidney function began to get better, a tiny bit at a time. After doctors had drained liters of fluid from his lungs, they were gaining the ability to function properly on their own. Even more encouraging, even though he was still dependent on a ventilator and a dialysis machine, Preston was beginning to respond to movement commands and seemed to be aware of conversations taking place around him, evident by a lifted finger or a squeeze from his hand.

Unexpectedly, doctors determined a couple of days later that he was stable enough medically to return to surgery for repair of his shattered left wrist. Dr. Donnelly explained to the Hammonds that he would be assisting Dr. Randall in surgery, with the intention to go in, explore the soft tissue, and see if there was any artery, tendon, or nerve injury visible to the naked eye. But because Preston was unable to communicate any neurological symptoms of feeling, or lack of feeling, he clarified that there could be repercussions to the nerves, due to the energy of the gunshot wound, even if the nerves appeared intact on visual inspection. The risks of this surgery, he explained, included infection and, most likely, the need for repeat surgeries, specifically bone grafting, due to the high energy of the fracture. It was time, however, to repair Preston's secondary bullet injury and allow it to heal.

In the operating room, the orthopedic surgeon, Dr. Amber Randall, and the accompanying team of medical professionals noted the bullet's entry wound on the larger of Preston's left wrist bones, the radius. It had exited on the underside of his wrist, along the direct radial border, before entering his chest. Astonishingly,

Preston's radial artery was completely intact, but the considerable force from the gunshot had fractured the bone into fragments. Doctors also discovered that much of the surrounding soft tissue in the palm of Preston's hand was in remarkably good condition. Furthermore, there was no visible evidence of nerve injury or tendon lacerations. The common question among us was, had the bullet ricocheted from the trunk of a ponderosa tree? Could that have been the reason it hadn't done more internal damage to his wrist or his lung?

One titanium plate and ten locking screws later, the medical team returned Preston to his quiet space in intensive care in stable condition, and reported to his family their amazement that the bullet hadn't done more internal damage upon entry. Dr. Donnelly, the attending surgeon, supported Dr. Randall's comments. Normally, he said, gunshot wounds require additional surgeries, but unless nerve function failed to return, Dr. Randall could quite confidently assure them that in this case, there may be no need for further surgeries.

Movement and warmth returned to my cousin's fingers and wrist just a few days after his second trip to the operating room. Even though he was still unable to speak, due to the tracheotomy, the medically induced coma was slowly being lifted and it was evident that Preston was now attempting to respond to his doctors' little physical commands more than before. His family would also receive small gestures from him, like a thumbs-up or a nod, when Preston was asked yes-or-no questions by medical staff.

CHAPTER 16

D ay after day, Brandon would visit Preston's bedside, not knowing if his brother could hear the encouragement coming from the voices of support surrounding him. Most of the time, Brandon continued to reflect on the past, often praying that positive progress would continue, always hopeful that a future full of new experiences with his brother would be possible. In a fogged weariness, his mind frequently cast back to their hunts and outdoor trips, and he yearned for a return to the uncomplicated part of their lives that he had, until then, taken for granted. More than anything, he wanted all of the past opportunities back—the hunts, the fishing trips, the boating adventures on Lake Powell. His brother and the outdoors were two prominent parts of his life, and he longed to return to the places where the two of them had shared endless hours, creating memories and stories that suddenly seemed a lifetime ago. Brandon thought about growing up as Preston's little brother, and remembered some of the inside secrets they'd shared during their youthful years. Nostalgia completely filled him when he thought about the way Preston had obtained his nickname, "Eagle," back in high school. The burden of guilt on his weary mind lightened a bit when he remembered his brother sharing the details.

It was Preston's freshman year at Page High School, the same school his mother had graduated from two decades prior as a varsity cheerleader. Determined to uphold her energetic status at school, Preston played on the football and baseball teams, proudly representing the Sand Devil's colors-red and black. But the stress of following in his mother's footsteps of admiration was overshadowed by the fear of the "tradition," a custom in the beginning of each school year. The tradition had prevailed for far longer than he could remember-one he never given much thought to growing up-until he began his Freshman year as an athlete. It was something none of his friends seemed to give much thought, something they never talked about while hanging out together. It was a ritual understood by all freshman boys on the football team. If a senior football player tagged a freshman player between classes, the freshman was forced to participate in the "naked run of shame" across the bridge which linked the town of Page to the Utah border. The event took place every fall, deep into the varsity football season, on a chosen Saturday night long after the clock had struck the curfew hour. On that designated night, all high schoolers who dared would sneak out of their bedrooms to either participate in or watch 'the run.'

The first two weeks of Preston's freshman year at the high-school were defined solely by fear. He sprinted from class to class without ever stopping to mingle with Collin or George or JD. When the after-school bell rang, he'd disappear from campus, the first to arrive on the football field for practice, afterwards sprinting home, without waiting for his friends- something had changed within my cousin, they feared. Eventually, one morning, a group of buddies he'd grown up with questioned him about his strange behavior on their walk to school. Guessing the reason for his strange behavior one of the asked, "What's the big deal? Why are you so scared about this? Preston knew that he'd eventually have to confess his reason for his fears. He knew that most of his buddies weren't worried for a good reason. Most of them were physically developing in places he wasn't. He avoided the subject long enough, so he blurted it out.

"I don't want to get caught," he confessed, "because I don't have any hair on my balls!"

Laughter erupted among the group. To hide his emotion, one friend covered his mouth and bent forward, as if upchucking, while slapping his knee. Two others offered each other high-fives, and a fourth kindly smacked Preston on the back of the head as a gesture of sympathy. "You're bald—like an eagle. We'll call you Bald Eagle," said one buddy, in a forcibly deepened voice that mimicked an Indian chief. The laughter and wisecracks continued the rest of the walk to school, where Preston was tagged moments before the first-hour bell rang.

As in all the years before, the customary run was scheduled to take place one predetermined, cold, fall night. Never before had crossing that one-thousand foot stretch of the bridge ever seemed so terrifying. Not once, even looking down the 700-foot drop, holding his mother's hand as a child, nor the many times crossing it with his dad for fishing tournaments on the lake, did he ever feel as vulnerable. The fear he felt that night about the bridge had never absorbed him, not even the first time he was behind the wheel driving across it, when he first received his driver's license. It was the lengthiest run imaginable. It was illegal, immoral—and "mandatory." It made Brandon smile to think about how it played out, but as he and the rest of the town lay sound asleep, more than a dozen freshman boys, including my slightly-underdeveloped cousin, Preston, darted their naked bodies across the finish line on that chosen Saturday night. When telling his story, Preston had mentioned to Brandon that he had increased his running speed that night, trying to keep up with the group of sprinters whose bodies masked his own. And he told him how the streakers were applauded and honked at from the start through the finish line. He'd remembered that the lengthy dash was accompanied by blaring music and high-beam headlights shining from the cars and trucks of the upperclassmen, who had lined up along the bridge's entrance to witness the midnight run. And he recalled the exhausted faces of all the participants at the finish line.

The fear associated with that occasion subsided after the following home football game, but the nickname remained. Eventually, his given name, "Eagle," became an acknowledgment of the everlasting, sincere friendship between Preston and his closest friends.

After thinking for a generous amount of time about the run that his brother had conquered back in high school, Brandon came up with an idea. He would slip away from the hospital that afternoon to purchase a pair of walking shoes; a pair, in his high-school colors that he could present to his brother one day, hopefully, as a gift of encouragement. He glanced at the monitors above Preston's bed that seemed to be energetically pumping energy and life back into his brother. He squeezed Preston's hand and whispered to him, "Come on 'Eagle,' you can do this."

CHAPTER 17

As Preston continued to slowly rebound from medical obstacles that had seemed impossible to defeat, doctors, therapists, and visitors continued to express their amazement at his ability to heal. After all, it wasn't every day that the trauma team and medical staff witnessed someone surviving internal damage to the chest from a high-powered hunting rifle.

The waiting area where we had initially gathered to offer support to the Hammonds and each other had been reassigned several times during the weeks following Preston's admittance, to accommodate the rise in the number of visitors to the intensive care unit. The room's atmosphere and the feelings among all of us remained mostly the same, though: cautiously optimistic. Supporters continued to bring small gifts and mingle among others rotating in and out of the hallways near the waiting area, which looked more like a makeshift temporary campsite, with pillows marking sleeping spots and blankets strewn among the cots and chairs. For long days that turned into weeks, we met there, anticipating the prospect of a possible resolution to the questionable recovery for Preston.

Occasionally, lightheartedness filled the otherwise somber space that was assigned to the Hammonds. This was especially true when Krista brought Jackson in to circulate with those visiting his daddy. The sight of him in his cowboy Christmas pajama pants carrying his wish list for Santa temporarily softened the surroundings. His innocence and energy helped things feel normal again, like they hadn't since the Thanksgiving holiday. And watching him proved to be a welcome break from the topics of conversation that generally maintained a common theme, contemplating my cousin's odds for the future.

In recent days, that topic only slightly wavered from the fear of survival to fears of the extent of his recovery. We listened closely as Brian or Camille recounted the straightforward facts of what Preston had overcome to that point, as well as where the future might lead him. Through our discussions with them, we learned that the volume of blood he lost on November 30 had plummeted him to the initial hypovolemic shock. And we began to understand how difficult that made it for his heart to pump sufficiently, and we sympathized with their concerns about his failing organs. We shared in the Hammonds' fear regarding the possible need for permanent kidney dialysis. And we comforted Camille as she feared his memory and speech would be altered. Most days now were filled with questions. For quite a while, there were few answers.

Between us, for days we talked about the obvious, the gunshot wounds to his chest and wrist, and asked ourselves and each other whether healing could ever be sustained. The 7-millimeter hunting rifle that Brandon carried the day of the hunt had the power to kill even the largest, heaviest game. It was the rifle of choice when the Hammonds hunted elk, especially bull. Those animals weighed in excess of 700 pounds and were routinely taken down by a single bullet. The bullet from a high-powered rifle of that magnitude could undoubtedly reduce blood vessels to dust and turn soft tissue into jelly in large game and humans. The same bullet could horribly splinter and fracture any bones that it came in contact with.

So how was it that the bullet that had pierced my cousin's wrist and chest hadn't torn through his vital organs? What kept the bullet completely intact after it was fired? What had caused it to lodge in his tailbone and skip the option to demolish his lungs and spine? How did the bullet's entry spare his wrist and arm from nerve and tendon damage? All that was reason enough to give thanks for the blessings of his ongoing life. It helped me realize that prayers were being answered and that God was working through the doctors and machines for Preston. He was indeed working in mysterious ways.

Yet impediments to the restoration progress continually recurred, as if reminding us that the fragility of Preston's life was still teetering. Another day of darkness presented itself shortly after his return to the operating room for wrist surgery. Through restlessness and distress, Preston jerked and turned, which caused him to fall from his bed—but once again, he escaped serious injury. It was devastating to hear that his arms would have to be fastened to the bed railings with straps, another form of confinement for him. I couldn't imagine the struggle my cousin must have been experiencing internally. He certainly had enough external obstacles to contend with.

Besides the physical struggle, he was mentally immobile as well. It was as if he was completely paralyzed, but experiencing a raging desire to be set free. My cousin was combative, and it was evident he wasn't going to let this accident destroy him. His inability to communicate verbally, along with his mental distress, left him weak and tired after bouts of struggling. He'd hardly made peace with his current circumstances, and it was clear that he wanted to defeat the barriers before him just as much as we all wanted him to. He was obviously using every resource within himself to prove that he was alive inside the confines of his situation. He wanted his family to know that he was fighting from within to return to them.

For days, he couldn't catch a break from regression. Shortly after the fall from his bed, a staph infection became an additional obstacle. Recognizing the magnitude of his internal struggle and the seriousness of this new infection, the attending doctors and Preston's family agreed to slow the procession of visitors to his room once again. He needed to maintain a serene environment to fight through the severity of his mental and physical injuries. At this point, it was between him and God; together they would work through *His* plan.

The December days continued to unravel with no visitation rights to Preston's quiet hospital room. Only his immediate family members were allowed to see and talk to him, and only one at a time. This regressive step backward in his progress was agonizing for them. For the rest of us, the disappointment meant the only means of communicating with him was through the Hammonds and CaringBridge.

As the serene winter days were marked on the calendar one at a time, my uncle Brian continued to read the entries and responses of concern softly to my cousin, keeping Preston and himself bonded with all of us in the world outside of theirs. The written reassurances were what Brian needed, now more than ever, as he sat hour after hour praying for small improvements to return. The messages were clear: no one was giving up. Paragraph after paragraph expressed hope that Preston was able to comprehend the encouragement coming from the homes and hearts of friends around the country, and family gathered near, and use its energy to further his healing process. At minimum, the words would inspire my uncle to remain vigilant in his copilot seat next to a captain who was flying into unknown territory.

The inspirations continued.

Preston and Family,

 I was looking at the blue sky a couple of days ago. Blue sky depends on which direction you are facing. You may see clear, blue sky, but you haven't turned around to see the stormy sky behind you. My friend, stormy skies are guided by God's hands...and "this too shall pass." You have been experiencing such an incredible recovery, we are ALL taken back when you experience a setback. I refuse to let my faith in GOD and in YOU down. Preston, I see blue sky all around!

Bambi G.

Another entry:

We had a beautiful day here in Virginia and a wonderful sunset this evening. The sky was full of reddish-orange clouds that brought to mind the gifts God gives us. It reminded me that we often take those gifts for granted, or we don't always appreciate them, until they are presented in the most meaningful ways. It also reminded me that life and the people in it change as time goes on, but their impressions are left on us that last a lifetime. You are one of those beautiful sunsets.

We love you,
Craig and Jo Ann

The following morning finally produced some good news that we'd all been waiting for. In fact, the next five days were highlighted with positives on my cousin's medical and physical roller-coaster ride. It was mid-December on the calendar, although the month had melted into an unknown quantity for the Hammonds. Preston's latest infection was subsiding, and he was awake now for short intervals each day. His physical therapist was working to help him regain movement and balance, and had him sitting in a chair next to his bed for short stints. A little at a time, his improving interactions with medical staff and his family were shown in his nodding and smiling. Finally, each new day was filled with positive energy and more interaction between Preston and his family.

CHAPTER 18

Preston's eyes rolled backward and then forward again as he struggled to make eye contact with Dr. Donnelly, who was standing over him during the early morning hours of December 17. Donnelly's assurances were heartfelt as he spoke to his fragile patient and the Hammond family. He could now confidently tell Preston that he was doing well medically and slowly, but steadily, making advancements, which he had once thought unimaginable. He spoke slowly and concisely to the room of tear-filled family members, who hung carefully on every word. Fighting to restrain his own emotion, he warned Preston that there could be more bad days ahead, but that mostly, moving forward, he believed they would be good. The road to recovery would be long and possibly filled with setbacks, but the healing, he assured Preston, was progressing positively. He momentarily directed his comments to the Hammonds, telling them to "keep doing whatever it is that you're doing." Each of them knew exactly what he meant. The power of their prayers was working.

Dr. Donnelly then asked my cousin if he understood what he was saying. The calculated upward and then downward tilt of Preston's head confirmed his understanding. When I heard about the conversation between my cousin and his trusted doctor, it was hard for me to comprehend how tough it must have been for him to process the validity of Dr. Donnelly's words. I wondered if he, too, had been scared about his future. I imagined he must have had time to come up with his own game plan over the past weeks, the one he would follow step by step to continue advancing. How would he gather the necessary strength within himself to keep improving? I wanted to know these answers.

As the elation of Dr. Donnelly's encouraging bedside report to Preston and his family faded, so, it seemed, did the forward motion of healing. Just two days after the euphoria, things seemed to plummet. Blood clots and further infection set in. Assuming their vigilant place of comfort and clinging to Dr. Donnelly's recent encouraging words, the Hammond family trudged forward in their faith, bathing in the continual encouragement and support from family and friends. They had an entire town pulling for them. In the hours and days to follow, it became clear that even the inevitable setbacks couldn't keep Preston or his family from walking with faith against fear.

That evening the following heartfelt message helped carry the Hammonds through a long day:

Dear Hammond Family,

I want to let you know that I have several priest friends around the country offering masses for you and for Preston this weekend. I have a good friend in Chicago who is a Reiki Master. She is sending healing energy to Preston. I have a couple of tribal leaders in the Houma Nation here in Louisiana doing a healing ceremony for him on Sunday evening in spite of the arctic cold-spell here. A Methodist Minister in New Orleans has added Preston to a prayer hotline at their church. I even have a Buddhist friend who is fasting for a day and offering prayers for Preston's recovery.

You have prayers being expressed in many forms and in many different faiths. I hope you can find some comfort in knowing you are surrounded by so much support and love, even from people you have never met. Please draw strength from their prayers during this time.

—Mark

My cousin didn't give up on things easily; ask anyone who grew up with him. It was apparent that after his discussion with Dr. Donnelly, he was determined to get through this situation, whatever it took. This fight for his life was for his brother, for his son, for his family, and then for himself. Had he been able to say something that day, it would have been an assurance to Dr. Donnelly that he was *"all in"* with his determination to heal fully. Within forty-eight hours, Preston would be weaned from the ventilator—forever.

Brandon frequented Preston's bedside for longer intervals each day now, whispering inspirations to his brother that no one else could hear. It was evident that he was counting on Preston, and vice versa, to pull through this time of uncertainty. The boys had a strong bond, and they would utilize it to get themselves far beyond this situation, one hurdle and one day at a time. Each of them would apply the dominant factors of his personality to carry the other forward: Preston, the more determined one, and Brandon more like Mim—quiet, but a spiritual warrior.

Mim had a gentle spirit, accepting of everyone she met. Although I would probably describe her as an introvert—someone who was most comfortable alone or beside Pip—she followed along in social situations as a quiet observer, leaving most of the mingling to my grandfather. She was a deep thinker whose demeanor made people feel comfortable in her presence. Her words were filled with measurable significance and gave me the confidence that I could achieve whatever I wanted to. Talking with Brandon had the same effect.

When we were kids, Mim taught us things that seemed insignificant at the time but now hold great meaning. I recall her mini-lessons on the value of good-quality walking shoes and her consistent reminders to carry sweaters with us, to ward off a chill, wherever we went. Her influences, on the surface, seemed like those of any empathetic grandmother. But Mim's advice was different. She taught by example—she walked her talk. She often instructed us not to hang on to things that weren't useful, as they quickly added up to clutter. In her mind, a cluttered environment was obsessive and wasteful. She also reminded us that people came into our lives for a reason and it was possible to learn something useful from everyone we met. Thinking back, her observations have held true throughout my life. Like Mim's, Brandon's words were few but meaningful during the weeks he spent beside his family in the hospital. He didn't let the confusion or the hindrances or the technicalities of Preston's condition derail his mission to support his brother through recovery, no matter how dire the process often became. When he and I would discuss the day's progress for a CaringBridge report, he jumped right to the facts, good and bad, offering no false hopes— no extra clutter.

I learned, when I became an adult, that Mim had experienced her own share of grief and loss. She had lost her youngest sister, Clara Bell, when she was a child. Clara Bell had drowned in a Michigan river at four years old. And Mim's father, Charles, also died prematurely. He had been involved in an accident too. As a fireman in 1934, he was working one frigid January night, when he slipped from the open back end of a fire truck as it crossed a set of railroad tracks on its way to an emergency call. Our parents had told us about those tragedies when we were kids, but I don't think I comprehended their impact until years later, when I watched Preston's unfold. Mim rarely talked about the loss of her father or her sister, and she never dwelled on any scarring those losses may have caused her. She was more attuned to the continual motion of moving forward in her life. Brandon was doing the same, looking at the future, continually pushing the obstacles placed before him into the background.

Seeing traces of Mim's personality in my cousin Brandon was comforting to me in recent weeks. The calmness in his voice helped me manage my thoughts about the possible outcomes for Preston, like the comfort of a sweater on a chilly evening. And with Brandon clearly focused on Preston's healing path, he was undoubtedly using some quality mental "walking shoes."

CHAPTER 19

In line with their continual spirit of giving and support for the Hammonds during the holiday season, employees at the west-side Home Depot store came through again with another way to brighten spirits, just a week before Christmas. This time their generous provision came in the form of good-natured gifts, lifting the sagging spirits of the Hammond family at Flagstaff Medical Center. The Hammonds would be spending the holiday in the intensive-care unit this year, so the team delivered some much-needed cheer.

More than a dozen of Preston's coworkers autographed orange aprons and scribbled good wishes and messages of motivation on the bibs. The aprons provided a vibrant touch to an otherwise colorless room that had become home to Preston and his family for almost a month. Their bright color brought new energy, like a morning's sunrise, and they hung proudly around the perimeter of Preston's bed. The messages written on those aprons, were like Christmas cards, and were read aloud to Preston and supplied him and his family the perfect gift of continued encouragement that was very much needed with each seemingly endless day.

With the kindness and support of employees, managers, and corporate personnel at the store, along with the excellent medical treatment and supportive prayers of his entire community, Preston was gaining the momentum he needed to progress with his physical condition in a positive manner, and optimism continued to replace fear among the Hammond family.

Time and rest were also proving to be good friends to Preston in his fragile state. A week before Christmas, Dr. Donnelly and a physical therapist again had my cousin sitting in a chair next to his bed, increasing the length and frequency as they concurrently weaned him from tubes and machines one at a time. An additional accomplishment occurred the same week, when the hemodialysis machine was removed from Preston's room. Its humming sound was suddenly absent. It was replaced with the sound of silence, which was both eerie and comforting. The machines that had kept Preston alive for weeks were crutches that the Hammonds depended on with each complication, but their absence provided a new sense of freedom that helped assure them that the doctor's prediction of progress was true.

For the first time since the accident, the Hammonds were feeling more confident about the future for Preston and for each of them. Dr. Donnelly's daily reports continued to reflect encouraging advances. Not only was he physically making progress, it now seemed likely that Preston would not be adversely affected mentally or neurologically by the extensive blood loss and nerve damage the gunshot caused. It was a report the Hammonds definitely weren't expecting one morning, when they were interrupted from laying their hands over Preston's chest in prayer. Amazingly, doctors now believed strongly that my cousin would merely experience subtle differences in personality, probably only recognizable by those closest to him.

That same evening, when Dr. Donnelly made his way to Preston's room during his rounds, he asked Preston to wiggle his toes. Without hesitation, Preston moved them a little and then lifted his leg slightly, exaggerating his response as if to replace words that would have reminded everyone that he was present, alive, and slowly finding his way back to normalcy. I'm sure everyone in the room was equally happy to witness Preston's physical advancements, but Brandon's smile radiated the brightest that evening. Finally, he was beginning to feel peace about the outcome of the accident. He heard the optimism he'd been waiting for in Dr. Donnelly's tone of voice, and now he had the opportunity to witness, first-hand, his brother's ability to follow commands. Preston was once again revealing his personality, the one Brandon had grown up with, hunted with, and loved. Brandon was not only getting his brother back, he was getting his best friend back too.

A few days before Christmas, doctors continued to test Preston's advancement physically and neurologically. An electronic voice box was placed over his tracheostomy. For the first time since he'd entered the emergency room nearly lifeless, he was asked to talk rather than nod. In response to the questions he was asked, Preston identified his wife. "Krissss-ta," he said, motioning toward her with his eyes. His words sounded sweet, coming from a mouth that had been quieted weeks earlier by a bullet. Hearing his own voice again made him emotional, and he began to cry. His senses and emotions were intact, providing complete relief to his family as they watched and listened attentively to his responses to inquiries about his surroundings. He continued to impress them, seeming to amuse medical personnel with answers that verified his mental capabilities. In response to the question, "Who is the other woman in the room?" He clearly pronounced his mother's name, "Camille."

The questions became more complex, directing him to remember recent events. He successfully answered a question regarding the most recent holiday. "Th-an-ks-givvving," he said. The Hammonds clapped with enthusiasm, encouraging him further. But exhaustion quickly ended the session and returned my cousin to a restful state of sleep. No greater gift could have been received that season. Cautiously hopeful, the Hammonds marched on, humbly sharing their experiences about Preston's advancements with family and friends. The prayer chains were working, they would tell visitors, as was Preston's momentum. His courage and healing power continued to define his medical outcome.

By now, the blood-clotting complications and lung function problems that had overwhelmed him rapidly began improving, while his kidneys were successfully, and suddenly, working on their own. For the first time in almost a month, the Hammonds' uncertainties were beginning to fade, and new plans were being discussed. The doctors were now talking about moving Preston out of intensive care and into rehabilitation within the week. Preston would need help with speaking and comprehension, and would need to relearn many tasks that the bullet had stolen from him—things that a month earlier would have been effortless: walking, talking, eating, swallowing, and digesting. And when he conquered all of those tasks and regained his strength and mobility, he could return to his home. Slowly, through extended therapy, he could start to put the pieces of his life back together.

News of the planned move from intensive care to the rehabilitation unit traveled quickly among hospital staff. Some of the personnel seemed as excited as the family was. The new information was the perfect reason for a celebration. One of the Hammonds' most cherished nurses, Jesse, came up with a great idea to honor the occasion of this fantastic update. He told Krista that he felt it was finally time to facilitate a visit between Jackson and his dad. It had been weeks since Jackson had seen his daddy. Krista had been mindful of the possibility of overwhelming either Jackson or Preston with visits during the first weeks in intensive care. She and Jesse had agreed that they would cue each other in when the appropriate time for them to see each other presented itself.

Krista had been waiting patiently for weeks for this opportunity to arrive. With careful preparation, Jesse arranged the visit for the two of them the following morning, when Preston was particularly rested, awake, and alert. Jesse and my uncle Brian carefully transferred Preston from his bed to a wheelchair, arranging the thin, unflattering hospital gown around his bandaged torso, and then carefully hid his thin legs and most of the tubes and sterile dressings beneath a blanket draped over his lap.

Brian slipped a pair of his favorite slippers onto Preston's bare feet and patted down the top and sides of his overgrown hair. Realizing that he would tire quickly, Jesse hurried Preston down the hallway in the wheelchair, greeting Krista and Jackson near the family waiting area. Both were still bundled in winter coats, Krista carrying a small, soft blanket over one arm and guiding little Jackson with the other. Jackson stood motionless in his knee-high snow boots, staring down the hallway toward his dad. Mother and son were evidence that the winter season was moving forward outside, and they were about to collide with the sparsely dressed, pale, and weakened reminder that life was on hold, still frozen in time, inside the intensive-care unit. It had been that way for far too long, since that last fateful day of the hunting season. The situation was complicated, frustrating, and encouraging for Krista all at the same time. It was the first time that Preston had left the confines of his private room in intensive care, and he was undoubtedly confused about his surroundings.

At first, the visit seemed a bit awkward, as neither Preston nor Jackson completely recognized the other. But slowly, Jackson began to warm up to his "Da-Da," offering him an additional flannel lap blanket and a sip of soda through a red plastic straw. The small group of visitors in the waiting area that morning, Nurse Jesse included, respectfully disappeared, making it possible for Preston to spend a few moments with Jackson and Krista, just the three of them, a family reunited. After they exchanged sentiments of affection, with encouragement and assistance from his mom, Jackson recited the alphabet and then softly kissed his Da-Da on the cheek before Nurse Jesse reappeared, interrupting the visit to return Preston to his room. The short time the three of them spent together was their first private visit, and Jesse promised there would be many to follow. Jackson now wanted to walk every step of the way through this journey with his dad. And the periods of time Preston was able to see Jackson, as they multiplied, seemed to feed his ability to grow a little stronger.

CHAPTER 20

I was back at our new home in the valley, working with my husband on last-minute gift wrapping and travel preparations for Christmas. We would be returning home to celebrate with our extended families in Flagstaff for the holiday, and that meant another opportunity to visit Preston. We anticipated seeing him much more often now because of his progressing healing advancements and his ability to interact with us. I was stuffing some warm winter sweaters into my suitcase as my husband, Richard, and I recounted the numerous improvements Preston was experiencing and how God was working through him to produce such a favorable outcome.

Richard reminded me how patience and persistence through prayer were really beneficial. I knew what he meant. He wanted me to make note of it and utilize the same concepts to better my own faith in my struggle to find happiness in our new city. He knew I was having a really tough time with the change, and the additional stress surrounding my cousin's accident had made the situation even more difficult. My dissatisfaction with our move from our hometown seemed whiny and unreasonable. I knew it appeared that way to my family too, so I tried to keep my regret buried deep within myself initially. That wasn't working very well, it was evident in my rising level of anxiety. I felt like God wasn't listening to me, and I wouldn't admit it openly, but I was angry with Him. For a couple of agonizing months, my family had watched me crumble emotionally.

In order to cope with everything going on around me, I kept myself as busy as I could, especially during the month of December, when my cousin was hospitalized. Besides our trips back and forth to Flagstaff, I had landed an exciting new position, writing articles and selling advertising for the monthly community newspaper. Interacting with individuals and businesses and the church in my new community was just what I needed to bring myself out of the slump I'd fallen into in recent months. And it picked me up even further to be able to pass on the new optimism my cousin was radiating from his hospital room through entries on CaringBridge. The continued outreach of supportive messages from around the country was inspiring. It was soul food for me to be able to write about the improvements Preston was making so close to Christmas, as Krista and Brandon continued to relay them to me over the phone. It was true, Preston was experiencing his "best days ever" just before the holiday, and I couldn't wait to get up north to be part of the excitement.

It was as if the Hammonds had obtained a fast pass to God's ear through their faith and prayer during the preceding weeks. More often each day, there was laughter coming from visitors in the waiting area and trailing in and out of Preston's room. Just prior to Christmas, the entries on CaringBridge poured in, and there were now more than 4,000 of them.

One of the messages Preston received just before Christmas was from his friend Chuck, who wanted him to know that his circumstance was an inspiration during the holiday season for *his* family. Chuck expressed how reading the entries on CaringBridge had become "viral" for him, as he imagined it had for so many others. He vowed to continue to follow Preston's story throughout his path to recovery. And he couldn't wait for the opportunity to have personal conversations with Preston again.

Another, from our cousin in Michigan, was especially meaningful; the message talked directly to me too.

Dear Camille,

I was so in touch with you this morning. As I prayed for all of my daughters and families, as they are racing about finishing up Christmas preparations, I thought about your vigil the bedside of your son. Oh, how hard it must be to sit and wait for every little sign of healing and recognition. The Lord is right at his bedside, with you. He is hearing the prayers and He will continue to heal Preston and restore him to you. His tragic accident is a lesson to us all to remember each day as a blessing, a glorious day unto our Lord. When we do that, we live in Him, as he wishes us to do.

Please know that I am praying for you as a Mother, no one can understand the hardship of sitting and waiting. Mary did.

—Donna

It was evident to me that when people pulled together in united devotion, their supportive actions helped not only the receiver of the intentions, but also those providing the messages to move forward in the healing process.

CHAPTER 21

The aroma of coffee hadn't yet penetrated the hallways in the acute care wing, but Brian was awake, staring at the muted TV's morning news, and Preston was slowly opening an eye, when Dr. Donnelly entered the room. It was going to be a challenging but rewarding day, he told my cousin as he glanced at the time on his wristwatch and then jotted notes on a clipboard. It was time for Preston to earn his way out of the intensive care unit and into the rehabilitation wing of the hospital. His ability to pass some physical and mental assessments would earn him the ticket he needed to make the transition. He felt that Preston's progression had improved enough to send him on to this next step toward recovery. In time, he explained, Preston would be returning home and ever so gradually regaining the lifestyle he'd experienced before the accident.

Dr. Donnelly retraced some of the advances Preston had recently achieved, saying that his liver and kidneys were improving, a bronchial scope showed improvement in the bacterial pneumonia, chest and lung X-rays looked favorable, he had spoken his first couple of words with the assistance of the voice box, and he adequately followed physical commands. In the very near future, he told Preston, his feeding tube would be removed and swallowing tests could be initiated. He added that it was important that Preston begin to get adequate nutrition, so he was going to have to learn to swallow foods again. Covering Preston's hand with his own, Dr. Donnelly praised my cousin for his bravery and diligence in his struggle to recuperate.

After experimenting with a tiny spoonful of applesauce and sips of juice, my cousin's swallowing function gradually returned to its pre accident state. This was good news. Another step in the right direction. Soon, it was time to introduce proteins, and for the first time in nearly a month, Preston was asked what he would like to eat. His first request for solid food was tuna fish. The sighs between the nurses and the Hammonds over this meal request were affectionately tossed around the room and were remarkable enough that Aunt Camille felt it should be noted in the *Footprints* journal. This menu choice seemed so far from anything Preston would ever choose to eat, she noted—but it was a turning point, a wonderful one. And just as rapidly as it had previously been robbed from them, joy filled the room and their spirits. There was teasing, joking, and laughter among them. It had been far too long since they'd laughed together, and I loved knowing it was happening again.

Two days before Christmas, nurses continued to encourage him to eat and drink a little more at each meal, in hopes of helping him regain some strength as well as some of the weight he had lost over the past month. He didn't seem very interested in eating much of anything, except tuna fish. So, if it was tuna fish he wanted three times a day, then that's what he'd get. A few bites here and there were all that he could manage, but it was another step to wellness. More important than the menu choice was the fact that he wanted to eat something, and the fish proved beneficial. Even the small bites were providing the energy to help him sit for longer periods each day.

With the assistance of nurses, he also began taking a few steps. Those few steps then turned into ten, and then from his bed all the way to the doorway. Each passing day offered momentum to be better than the last. Spontaneously one evening, Brandon grabbed a wheelchair from the hallway and helped Preston into it. With Camille, Brian, and Krista not far behind, he pushed his brother to a window that revealed snowflakes gently falling outside. *Should we?* Preston watched in amazement as the heavy doors slowly opened, and the brisk, chilly winter air brushed across his cheeks as his family wheeled him outside for just a couple of moments. Preston gazed across the parking lot in wonder as pillows of snow piled on the branches of ponderosa pine trees. He stared as if seeing them for the first time. The pinkish sky and quiet of the falling snowflakes seemed magical to all of them. The Hammonds stayed outside long enough to collect snowflakes on their eyelashes that quickly dissolved among their warm tears of happiness. The snow seemed to trickle happily through the air as if to join in the celebration of the return of my cousin's life.

CHAPTER 22

On Christmas Eve, the Hammond family paid a return visit to the hospital's small chapel, little Jackson included, to pray for Jackson's Da-Da. The small, quiet sanctuary was the place each of the Hammonds had returned to often in recent weeks, beginning with the first evening following the accident, for solitude and clarity. It quickly became a place of security they could go to, together or individually, when the doctors' reports and the infections and setbacks became too much for them to endure.

Jackson took his turn that evening, kneeling on one of the two kneelers, guided by his mommy, while my aunt Camille stood next to him as they prayed, holding a single white candle she'd lit upon their entrance. This Christmas Eve was different from any other in the past. No service with familiar seasonal hymns to sing along to, no formal prayers echoing responses from familiar fellow parishioners, no references to the night in Bethlehem. This year, it was just a small family, gathered in *His* name, to give thanks for the gift of life that had been renewed to their very own son, brother, husband, and dad. That night, the Hammonds had the small sanctuary, highlighted with a colorful stained-glass window, all to themselves, so they were able to pray openly among one another.

Together, they prayed for patience in the physical and mental healing process ahead for Preston, and offered their thanks for the peace that was filling their recently troubled minds. That evening marked a turning point for each member of Preston's family. They decided that it was time to leave behind the circumstances and complications of the accident. If the details simmered within any of them for much longer, it would interrupt their ability to thrive as a family in the future, they agreed. From that point forward, they vowed to anticipate the positive aspects of what the coming days would bring and promised not dwell on what the accident had taken away. At the conclusion of their time in the chapel that evening, each of them agreed to completely accept whatever the future would bring.

After their prayer session in the chapel, they made their way back through the hallways that had been quieted by the holiday to check on Preston, who was sleeping soundly. They would spend the next couple of hours away from his bedside, visiting with local family and friends, sharing desserts and stories about past Christmases as well as updates regarding Preston's most recent medical advancements.

When he arrived back at the hospital several hours later, Brian returned promptly to Preston's room, and Camille and Brandon followed, after helping Krista tuck Jackson into bed at their home. Brian brushed his hand across Preston's forehead, whispering to him that it was Christmas Eve and that a bright future was highly anticipated for him in the upcoming new year. There was no answer from beneath the white cotton blanket covering Preston's fragile body. But the sound of his son breathing quietly in sleep, unassisted by any machine, made the world feel softer and more beautiful than it had before. He then situated himself in the recliner next to Preston's bed, as he had for many nights, threw a blanket around his shoulders, stared up at the ceiling, which was dimly lit by light filtering in from the hallways that never slept, and reviewed the events of the evening in his mind.

He thought about past Christmases, years ago, when the boys were young. He remembered about the shift work and long hours at the power plant and how he sometimes raced home early on Christmas morning to share in the excitement when the boys woke up. He remembered how the season used to seem stressful to him, and how he left most of the pre-Christmas preparations for the boys and around the house to Camille, because of his anxiety over gift shopping. He recollected how Christmas changed as the boys entered their teen years, and he almost laughed out loud when he recalled one particular white Christmas when he and Camille gathered the boys and picked up their cousin Ryan to play in the snow. He had driven them to the town's airport parking lot to spin circles—donuts, the boys called them—all Christmas afternoon.

The Page airport would have been the perfect place for that kind of fun. The small municipal runway serviced mostly private planes and chartered flights to surrounding areas like the Grand Canyon, Phoenix, Las Vegas, and St. George, Utah. My uncle had a way of bringing out the best of the activities in their small town, and that day the runway was theirs. It was small-town living at its finest.

It made him smile that night to think about Preston, even at twelve years old, being adamant about the rule of only opening *one* gift on Christmas Eve, and that the contents of the boys' stockings were always savored and saved as the last gifts opened on Christmas morning. He remembered the many Christmases spent at Mim and Pip's house in California in the boys' teen years, and he could envision Mim preparing a ham and Pip concentrating on perfecting his famous fudge recipe, making sure half the mixture included walnuts, the other half none. He could almost see a kitchen and living room filled with the cousins and uncles and aunts of his boys, laughing as they caught up on their lives, what each of them had accomplished, where they had visited, anything and everything since the previous year. And he drifted into sleep thinking about his satisfaction over how the years had unfolded for his family. It was comforting to remember how the boys had returned home every year as adults to reunite with him and my aunt. He was proud of the way the boys made a point of catching up with their high-school and college buddies, who would also return home to Page for the holidays. And he enjoyed watching his boys interact with each other as grown-up kids.

"Merry Christmas," he whispered to my aunt Camille, who had positioned herself in a chair across the room, where she wrote about the evening's events in her journal. Her Christmas Eve journal entry noted her admiration for Brian, a father so committed to his family, and how much it meant to her to see him so devoted to his son. Before the clock struck the midnight hour, Camille slipped out of the hospital room and returned to Preston and Krista's house to spend a warm Christmas Eve. It was the first night since before the hunting tragedy that my aunt and uncle would sleep soundly, without interruption.

I couldn't help thinking of it as true. Mim and Pip would have honored Preston's improvements and the eve of Jesus's birth the very same way the Hammonds were that evening. They would have privately prayed in the chapel and then continued through the evening by attending traditional celebrations, with humble appreciation for their blessings, never looking back long enough to consider themselves victims of circumstance. They would have embraced the importance of gathering with family in celebration of the season. Aunt Camille had been raised with those same beliefs, and she practiced them still. I can almost hear Mim's whispers through Camille's voice, assuring herself, in reference to their hardship, "This too shall pass." That evening, the Hammonds were simply the vessels carrying out my grandparents' lifelong legacy of faith under any circumstances.

CHAPTER 23

Christmas morning began like most recent mornings in the intensive care unit, with a routine shift change for Preston's nurses and an examination and assessment with a therapist, as Uncle Brian quickly rose from his chair, tucking his flannel shirt into his jeans, as if he'd slept through some of the magic of Christmas morning. It had been almost a month since he'd slept so soundly, and frankly, he had a lot of rest to catch up on. He knew this would be the day, the one he had been anticipating over the past week. He had carefully prepared exactly what he would say to Preston, over and over in his mind.

He listened carefully as doctors told Preston that, assuming he was feeling up to it, he could anticipate some family time with Krista and Jackson later that morning, but first a few details about the accident needed to be discussed. It was time to determine whether Preston had any recollection of the events of the last day of November. Did he know where on his body he was injured? Did he realize he'd been shot? And who was present at the accident scene? The medical professionals listened closely to Preston's answers, as did each of the Hammonds. How much did he know about what had happened to him that day?

After those questions, most of which Preston had no answers for, and following a short physical examination, all of the medical staff cleared the room, leaving just Preston and Brian. Leaning in closer to the bedside, Brian began the conversation that he had been rehearsing for the past week. He first promised Preston that future Christmases would be at home, adding ideas of how he thought those holidays might unfold. He then asked Preston if he wanted to know the basics of his accident. Preston nodded. He wanted to know.

Slowly tracing his index finger around Preston's wrist and then in a circular motion around his upper chest, Brian showed Preston the points of the bullet's entry on top of his bandages. Brian explained that he had been accidently hit by Brandon's bullet, and told him how long he had been in the hospital. Preston looked blankly at his dad, as Brian continued to discuss the unfolding events of November 30, of which Preston seemed to have no recollection. He told Preston the doctors had lost him three separate times on the operating table the day he was brought in. And he reminded Preston how blessed he was to be able to speak to him that day. This was a day Brian feared would never come, he told Preston.

The two of them cried together, and in a weak, broken voice, Preston told his dad that he felt sorry for Brandon. He wanted to know how Brandon was holding up and if he was doing okay. Brian reassured him that he was, mentioning also that he and Camille had watched his actions very closely over the weeks following the accident. Brian explained that Brandon had been suffering a great deal emotionally because of what had happened. Preston asked his dad to tell Brandon that everything was going to be okay, he was going to get through this, and to remind him that he loved him.

After a few moments' pause, Preston asked Brian, "Did we get the elk?"

"No," Brian responded.

Preston wiped his eyes and broke out in a soft laugh, verifying to Brian that everything was going to be as it once was. Preston was indeed able to comprehend again. The morning had revealed a great deal of information and emotion for both of them. It was a conversation Brian told me he would never forget. During their extended Christmas morning talk, Preston and Brian agreed that someday, the three hunters would return together to the scene of the accident, for closure. They also agreed that they would not allow the accident to keep them from hunting together again in the future. Their relationship and their outdoorsmanship were two of the things that defined the Hammond boys, and that's the way it always would be in the future, they decided.

In conclusion, the seriousness of their discussion gave way to something much more lighthearted, similar to the way the two of them had joked with each other prior to the accident. Together they continued to recollect and make future plans for quite a while that morning, uninterrupted by anyone outside of the hospital room. My uncle told me later that it felt great to be able to have a conversation like that again with Preston. There had been some uncertainty over whether he would ever get the opportunity.

After the father-and-son discussion, Preston attempted a few bites of pancakes and sausage that had been delivered to his room unnoticeably during their conversation. This was a Christmas breakfast that Nurse Jesse encouraged him to eat, if he ever wanted to regain his strength and get out of that place, as he explained it. Preston was stubborn about not wanting to eat much of anything, but Jesse was persistent with his appeals, explaining that the nutrition was something his body greatly needed to aid in his recovery. He reminded Preston that he had a long, long way to go in order to become physically stable again.

Brian snuck away briefly during Preston's breakfast and called Camille. He asked her and the rest of the family to hurry to the hospital. They would be in for a surprise, he promised. When they arrived, Preston greeted them, freshly showered. It was as if the morning's conversation with his dad and the bites of Christmas breakfast had given him a boost of encouragement and physical stability. Although he appeared weak, he had no tubes protruding from his torso or neck, which was an advancement Krista had not yet seen. His throat was merely covered with gauze and surgical tape. Even more surprising, he was talking somewhat normally when his family arrived.

As my uncle Brian described it, the best part of Christmas Day that year was witnessing Preston walk a few steps from his wheelchair down the hallway from his room in acute care, to see his wife and son waiting to greet him. For a few hours that morning, Krista, Jackson, and Preston exchanged gifts in an empty waiting room, sharing interactive time together for the first time in a long time. They talked mostly about the gift of the beloved support system and the gift of life, which now had more meaning than ever to each of them.

Late that afternoon, Richard and I had an extended Christmas visit with Preston. This time, it felt so encouraging to see him and be able to interact with him more than we had in recent weeks. The atmosphere surrounding those around him had lightened, and everything associated with his future seemed much happier too. Seeing him that day was definitely a gift for us. At first, we couldn't help but focus on his chest, which was covered in wrappings and bandages, reminders of the physical wounds that were slowly beginning to heal. And the white gauze and medical tape covering the opening in his neck where the tracheotomy had been closed couldn't be missed either, but his excitement about being able to communicate with us overshadowed the bruising and bandages.

He was pale but alert, and he was anxious to show off his ability to talk. We made it a point to listen, rather than ask him any questions that day. At times during our visit, I wasn't sure exactly what he was talking about, but his soft words sounded soothing, with a voice that had been quieted for too long. He was obviously still experiencing some confusion about recent incidents and the details of his hospital stay, and he had some weight to gain back, but for the most part, my cousin looked and sounded more like himself than he had in more than a month. His enthusiasm to communicate with visitors that day was inspiring.

It was a reassurance to me that he was sorting through things, getting through this ordeal one step at a time. I knew he wanted to talk about the weeks he'd lost while in a coma (he mentioned it), but his thoughts changed quickly from one topic to the next. He was clear about how grateful he felt to be loved by so many supporters. He also expressed his gratitude to the staff at Flagstaff Medical Center for the care he was receiving. He wanted all of us surrounding him that afternoon to thank the intensivists and continue to praise their efforts. Looking back, that Christmas revealed some of the best gifts we'd ever received. The whole progression of Preston's physical situation, and the way it brought extended family and community together, remains especially meaningful for me. If I'd never paused enough to savor my blessings, that Christmas Day I definitely did.

When it was time to leave that afternoon, we hugged him and told him that we would continue follow each of his recuperation steps. He acknowledged our promise with a nod and whispered that many people were counting on him to get back to his life, and he didn't want to let any of them down. It was evident that his outstanding will to live had helped carry him to this point. I couldn't wait to return to my laptop that evening to update all of his remote supporters, the ones who had not yet experienced Preston's awareness, as I did, on Christmas Day. Aunt Camille and I agreed that for the first time, the CaringBridge update should be cheerful and express the new feelings of joy surrounding Preston's situation. It seems silly looking back now, but I followed her direction and put a quirky twist on the poem "'Twas the Night Before Christmas," combining the spirit of Christmas with my spirit of gratefulness. It went like this:

> 'Twas the night before Christmas,
> And all through the hospital
>
> Not a creature was stirring
> Not even a spouse.
>
> The orange Home Depot aprons hung by his bedside with care,
> In hopes that our Preston would soon be working back there.
>
> While Jackson was nestled all snug in his bed,
> With visions of his daddy coming home soon dancing in his head.
>
> And Krista with her blanket and Brandon in his cap,
> Had just settled down for a long winter's nap.
>
> When what to our wondering eyes should appear,
> But a wonderful doctor, friends and family so dear.
>
> One day in his room, there arose such a clatter,
> He sprang from his bed, to see the snow scatter.
>
> Away to the window he flew like a flash,
> Tore away from that tubing, wanted outside in a dash.
>
> The moon on the breast of the new fallen snow,
> Gave a luster of midday to FMC down below.

I peeked in the window, saw Preston one night
A stubborn young man, not quite jolly or mellow
When it came time for food, he wanted tuna, not Jell-O.

He spoke not a word, but went straight to his work,
He had healing to do, fixing every quirk.

I saw his thumbs-up, and I know he might say,
Merry Christmas to all—please continue to pray!

It must have been all of the excitement of Christmas Day, visiting with his family, the gifts, and the time spent with Krista and Jackson that made him plunge again. December 26 turned out to be one of those projected bad days among the good ones that Dr. Donnelly had discussed with Preston earlier that week, but this time it had the Hammonds alarmed.

Preston hadn't slept well on Christmas night. He was restless, even vomiting, and his blood pressure shot up to dangerous levels again, just as it had right after his initial surgery. The attending doctors determined that they needed a scan of his brain and an ultrasound of his kidneys and bladder to determine what was going on. The day took on a somber disposition, and Krista, Camille, Brian, and Brandon resumed their patience and positions at the hospital as they watched Preston sleep most of the day and into the evening, praying for his positive momentum to return. Sighs of relief blanketed the room when, thankfully, all reports came back favorable early that evening. This time the setback was blamed on pure exhaustion or something viral.

Preston woke up late in the evening to the voices of the Hammonds talking quietly to each other. As quickly as he had gone spiraling downward, he ascended again. After a day filled with tests and hours of sleep, he was hungry, and asked for something to eat. With the approval of his attending nurse, Brandon and Camille slipped out for a fast-food run. They returned with a double cheeseburger, fries, and a chef salad, helping Preston eat a few bites of each. It was food, real food, and Camille's journal entry remarked on the pleasure of seeing Preston's appetite erase their early morning doubts about his condition. That day's incident turned out to be the last extreme regression Preston would experience before being transferred out of intensive care. "It was a happy night," Camille noted. "Just another obstacle that Preston has overcome. Thank God."

CHAPTER 24

By December 27, after his dramatic course in the intensive-care unit, Preston's condition had improved sufficiently enough to allow his transfer to inpatient rehabilitation. "You've outstayed your welcome," Dr. Pedersen told Preston jokingly on the morning he was wheeled from the acute care unit. For those of us watching from outside, some of the earlier uncertainties of his life didn't seem nearly as frightening now. Behind closed doors, however, Preston's struggle to regain his strength and health were ongoing.

There were turning points and milestones in his recovery process to be praised, as well as many hours and days of hard work for him yet to endure. There were lessons for each of us who had followed the events of the past month to take away from his accident, wisdom about dealing with uncertainty. There were unexplainable medical advancements to recognize and examples of personal determination to observe. Still, it was evident that Preston needed our continued support to help carry him through the recuperation process, no matter how long it might be. His battle hadn't yet been won. My cousin and his family had a lot of work to do in order for Preston to become independent again.

The new surroundings offered fresh hope for progress that would eventually become a part of Preston's personal history, a period of their lives that the Hammonds would never forget. The transfer from the solitude of his single bed in the ICU to a private rehabilitation room included new equipment and a team of therapists with new tasks. Preston participated in physical, occupational, and speech therapy several times a day for a week.

This new atmosphere was completely different from where he'd been, lying practically motionless and in silent surroundings in previous weeks. The carpeting in the new wing of the hospital had color, unlike the shiny, sterile gray tile of the intensive-care unit. The hallways had more movement, more voices, even laughter, which now sounded like unfamiliar background noise to my cousin. A variety of visitors and medical professionals scurried to and from rooms and gathered at and dispersed from the nurse's station opposite the humming elevator. His new environment was faster paced, which proved to be another significant challenge in his recovery.

When he first arrived, he was weak and required assistance to get out of bed and engage in even the lightest activities, like sitting, eating, and taking a few steps. It's as if his progress had taken a few steps of its own—backward. He also had notable memory and perception impairments when tested initially, another area in which he seemed to regress from just three days earlier. I imagined that it must have been incredibly difficult for Preston to adjust to this new situation. After making unbelievable advancements in intensive care, he must have become comfortable in the controlled, familiar environment. He would have to overcome his anxiety about this new place that presented new specialists, new tests, new barriers to overcome. He would have to rebuild his plan within himself all over again, to move forward with recovery. How would he overcome this newest set of fears?

With the new environment came new challenges. For five days, Preston worked himself to exhaustion to pass hurdles for the doctors, nurses, and physical therapists in his quest to become rehabilitated. My cousin continued to strive to remove the physical barriers set before him, often becoming frustrated with his lack of judgment and impulsivity. He didn't quite look like the Preston we had all known before the accident.

That fateful November morning had robbed him of more than thirty pounds. His hair was longer than we'd ever seen it, and his eyes appeared sunken in the paleness of his slender face. His right arm remained in a splint throughout his stay in the rehabilitation facility, but his tracheotomy incision and the surgical wounds on his chest and back were clean and healing favorably beneath the wraps and bandages that covered much of his torso. Ever so slowly, Preston was healing physically and mentally from being secluded, finding his way through new paths of uncertainty, and so were each of the Hammonds.

By December 28, a physical therapist had Preston walking for short intervals down the hallway at various times of the day. In between walks, he was spending more time in a chair, although the vertical movement caused him to be weak and dizzy. The short walks and sitting sessions were repeated several times a day, as Preston could tolerate. Seemingly now each day brought positive advancements, and it was a pleasure to be able to report them on CaringBridge. Additionally, that day the sutures were removed from Preston's right wrist.

The meetings between the medical doctors, the therapists, and the Hammonds regarding the hard work ahead sometimes became overwhelming in the days following Preston's move to the rehabilitation unit. It became clear that in order to help care for Preston, each of the Hammonds would have to agree to take care of themselves too. Attempting to do just that, Brian broke away from the hospital one evening, long enough to take little Jackson for a drive around the neighborhood to look at Christmas lights prior to the new year. Brandon paused from his vigil at Preston's bedside for a couple of days in order to check in at work and his home in the valley, updating concerned coworkers and gathering his mail. Camille and Krista took Jackson on short food and ice-cream runs during different times of the day and night, to breathe the clean mountain air and circulate among people outside the hospital setting.

Meanwhile, Preston continued working hard to achieve small goals placed before him by the medical professionals. Bigger goals were quick to follow the smaller ones. Soon, it was determined, he needed to practice using a wheelchair. When he mastered riding down the hallway, he was instructed to practice pushing the wheelchair, then he needed to be able to put the chair in the car and take it out, with family assistance, which earned him a day pass home. Finally, he could sit in the familiar surroundings of his living room and savor a nap in his own bed. The joy of his day pass quickly turned to sorrow when he was returned to the hospital to be monitored for the night.

During his days of rehabilitation therapy, Brandon could talk with Preston for however long his brother deemed comfortable that day. They talked about past holidays and shared stories that they both seemed to enjoy all over again. It was gratifying for Brandon to see his brother taking interest in small but significant recollections of their shared past. Even better, Preston was adding details to their stories, validating that his long-term memory was intact. Theirs was a bond that had been fractured, but not broken. It was now evident that their future would include further adventures together.

The world as they once remembered it was revealing itself slowly to them. Brandon had endured each and every day of the painful recovery process with his brother. He had spent every hour wondering and praying that this day would come. He couldn't re-member feeling as encouraged as he felt about Preston's memo-ry since hearing the positive tone in Dr. Donnelly's voice weeks earlier, when he talked about the possibility of a good outcome. Brandon couldn't ever imagine life without his brother, and now he wouldn't have to.

Almost a week after Christmas, Camille and Brian showed signs of mental relief regarding Preston's condition and were beginning to focus on the future again. Brian began to take phone calls, and was often seen pacing with his cell phone among the medical professionals in the hallways of the rehab unit. Some of his calls were from family and friends he hadn't spoken to in over a month. Others were from people at work giving updates and messages of encouragement. He was finally making plans to return to his duties at the power plant. He was eating regularly, and laughter occasion-ally returned to his conversations. Life was unfolding kindly, with assurances that it would return to some semblance of normalcy.

Aunt Camille was planning things again for herself and her family, and that was a sign that she was healing too. It was unusu-al for a holiday season to conclude without her homemade white chocolate–covered peanut-butter cookies, or her organizing a fam-ily new year's skiing excursion. That year, I felt assured that she'd happily continue her traditions and would soon be making plans for next year.

Camille, at her core, is an optimist, like Pip was. And when I miss him sometimes and long for the joy he brought to everyone in our family and around him while in this world, I see hints of him in my aunt Camille. She carries on his legacy by continually reaching for the positive possibilities of the future, forever organizing what comes next, not only for herself, but for her friends and extended family members too. Just like Pip, she's always had a natural ca-pacity to strike up conversation with others, knowing just the right thing to say to validate someone's needs and feelings; people seem to like that about her. I believe this is one of the reasons that she has always naturally maintained a close relationship with her boys.

From the time they began to walk and talk, Camille nurtured their emotional intelligence through acknowledgment and encouragement, which helped them gain lasting friendships with others as they grew up. She succeeded over the years by avoiding gender-stereotypical activities during their youth, and encouraged them to participate in social events that weren't just for girls, as she would tell them, like bake sales and community-service projects. This ultimately brought out the qualities of appreciation and respect for their mom and all the women in their lives. And even now, as grown-ups, her boys maintain strong bonds with their mother.

Krista could finally encourage Preston about his return home. Soon, she told him, he wouldn't have to return from a day pass. Soon he could come home again for good. It was no longer a question of if, but when. After taking thousands of small steps down a long, complicated medical road, it was time to take leaps in the area of mental stability so Preston could earn his way back to it. Krista helped him regain perception and mental clarity skills by asking him questions from a sports-trivia game, one of the gifts they received during his hospital stay. The late-evening board-game sessions in the rehab unit encouraged cognitive exercise, bettering his perception skills. Krista was surprised by some of his answers, especially when he blurted them out correctly, as he'd done at game nights with their friends prior to the accident.

On the last day of the year, Preston took a marathon walk down the hallway and back. His persistence during the grueling physical therapy sessions was paying off. Preston and his team of doctors and therapists couldn't be more pleased with his medical and physical advancements. Somehow, word of his developments grabbed the attention of the media. The local newspaper interviewed my uncle about Preston's outstanding recovery.

CHAPTER 25

January first marked a new year on the calendar, as well as a new beginning for my cousin. By seven thirty that morning, he had fully dressed himself, head to toe. After tying the laces of the walking shoes Brandon had placed with his belongings, he continued asking arriving family members, "What do I need to do to get out of here?"

The process to become healthy again seemed at times like an eternity to my cousin and his family. Preston wanted nothing more than to go home. All the therapy and medical tests had concluded that there was no need to keep him hospitalized full time any longer. Happily, this day marked a new foundation for the entire Hammond family. New Year's Day offered new expectations and optimism for positive outcomes and for reasons to continue to have faith. For me, it was a day of understanding that faith works not *for* us, but *through* us. I had watched over the past month as family and friends pulled together to support, love, and pray for God's will. That New Year's Day, I was reminded of the strength and power of all those prayers. Preston's is a true story of beating all odds. It's important for me to acknowledge the ways that faith united so many lives over a month's time.

After thirty-two painstakingly difficult days, Preston Lee Hammond, accompanied by his wife, Krista, and son, Jackson, walked out of the Flagstaff Medical Center after being shot in the wrist and chest with a high-powered 7-millimeter hunting rifle. The steps out the front door of the hospital that day were the stepping stones of great achievement, steps that eventually led to the return of his independence. It was that very special day, that Preston earned his walking shoes. I knew then, that it must be true – an Eagle must first walk before he can fly. That phrase of endearment had been tossed around among us during his stay at the medical center.

Nonetheless, the first day of January was a huge breakthrough in Preston's physical progress. Walking felt more incredible to him than it had the days before—this time his steps were leading him home. He wasn't quite the same person who entered the medical center a month prior, but was still striving to move forward in every area of his restoration. In recent weeks, his entire world had transformed from dull and colorless to bright and vibrant in anticipation of each day ahead. New Year's Day was celebrated as a new transformation of Preston's life, rather than a reflection of the devastation of the past month. There was no space in the Hammonds' minds to imagine the way things could have been had the odds prevailed.

On New Year's Day, my CaringBridge journal entry included the following words, which were written to encourage all the people who had supported and encouraged the Hammonds through those thirty-two painstaking days. I wrote:

Can you believe in miracles? Now, I can. When I hear his voice—talking and laughing again, it brings tears to my eyes. I can't imagine how life might have been for Krista, Jackson, Camille, Brian, and Brandon without Preston. He is truly a New Year's inspiration for us all. Preston reminds me that our circumstances are not luck—they are blessings!

On January 2, my uncle Brian concluded his updates on CaringBridge, turning the page to the next chapters in their lives. He wrote the following heartfelt message to followers:

> This is Brian, and I am back in Page this week. I plan on returning to Flagstaff for the weekend to be with Preston, Krista, and Jackson. Returning to work was difficult for me. It was important to me to be with Preston for every step, every therapy session, and every long night, in case he needed me to lean on. But, he's encouraged me to take a few steps of my own—steps to forgiving myself and steps that will help put my life back into a forward motion. It will be good for all of us to get back to the way it used to be. Preston is doing well and Camille, Krista, Jackson, and Brandon are with him today. I cannot quite put my thoughts into words, but I want to thank each and every person for their prayers. God is good, and he does listen. The support for Preston has been tremendous. Our entire family has been touched by the Lord during this time of great need. God will continue to be the focus of our lives for all eternity. We continue to pray for Preston's full recovery, as well as for his return to a normal daily routine. God bless you all and thank you so very much.

As the succeeding days and weeks continued, so did the endless follow-up appointments for Preston. It's been said that nothing good comes easy, and that certainly held true for my cousin as he continued for months to become the same physical and mental person he was previously. Although most of his friends and our extended family members had returned to their work routines and business as usual in their personal lives, Krista, Camille, and Brandon remained diligent in their support, alternating with personal care of Preston at home, keeping up with his medications,

changing bandages, and chauffeuring him to and from his therapy and medical appointments.

At first, he was required to attend daily therapy sessions, which
were designed to help him with some of the basics, including the
reintroduction of solid foods, adequate nutrition to support his
healing, and physical therapy to help improve his motion and
mobility. There were medications to be weaned from. There were
wounds, both physical and mental, to rectify.

In addition, Preston needed assistance with his cognitive
health; being able to problem-solve was tedious and difficult for
a while. There were tests to help with logic, comprehension, and
his capability to reason. The lists of tasks, at times, seemed never-
ending. Many sessions began with Preston verbalizing to therapists
that he easily became frustrated. Tasks during therapy added to
his irritation. The first task might be to change seats in the room
in a certain order, which he could accomplish with 100 percent
accuracy, but his ability to focus would quickly deteriorate. When
asked next to identify a new story played on a CD, Preston could
only do so with 50 percent accuracy. And his frustration would
build when he was asked to recall the details of a picture placed
before him.

Gradually, as Preston progressed, he was able to complete various memory, word finding, speech, and computer tasks with 97
percent accuracy, so the therapy sessions were reduced to three
times per week, and then once a week, and then once a month.
With ongoing support and assistance from his family, friends, and
coworkers, Preston returned to work at the west-side Home Depot
store as an assistant store manager on August 6, nine months after
the shot was fired that nearly claimed his life. His dream of man-
aging his own store was buried deep within his memory.

CHAPTER 26

Life was steadily returning to a state that the Hammonds considered normal. Krista, although exhausted mentally from her bedside watch during Preston's critical-care weeks, could finally focus more on being a mother to Jackson, with the help of her mother, who stayed with her for days at a time during the first few months of the new year. Aunt Camille made frequent trips from Page to Flagstaff, to help Krista and Preston care for Jackson too. For months, there were mountains of medical paperwork to be organized, insurance claims to file, and bills to be paid. She helped ease the burden of cooking, laundry, and cleaning during the weekdays when my uncle was at work.

Brandon continued to be within conversational reach of his brother via frequent cell-phone calls. He had returned to work and his home in southern Arizona, and visited Preston frequently on weekends. The two of them often had lengthy conversations about Preston's physical progress and the trials and tribulations of his therapy sessions. Brandon's support never wavered. He brought his own life back into balance by remaining engaged in every step of Preston's rehabilitation. Brandon knew his brother's life had become immobilized by his mistake and couldn't get past his own paralyzing guilt over being responsible for what happened. He realized during the first months following Preston's release from the hospital that *he* was going to need his brother's support as much as Preston needed his.

They agreed that they had a great amount of discussion to catch up on regarding the events of the day that dramatically changed both of their lives. But they spent the majority of their time focusing on where their paths in life might take each of them moving into the future. Their father had reluctantly returned home, to the routine of his supervisory duties at the power plant in Page. But he returned to Flagstaff on weekends to assist with duties around the house and to enjoy being surrounded by the people most important in his life again.

I, too, had put the events of the holiday season behind me and was working through faith to gain momentum for an optimistic new year. One particular day, I was trying to secure advertising leads for the community newspaper, and with the help of the quick pace of monthly deadlines and the assurance that my cousin was recovering successfully, I was beginning to settle into new opportunities in my new desert surroundings, when my cell phone rang. It was Preston calling.

Because I wasn't expecting it, I was startled by the ring and the interruption in the busy morning, as I stared into a list of advertising contacts on my computer screen. It was Preston's agenda that day to reach out to each of us who had made an impact on his journey to recovery. I stood up from my desk, walked away from it, and smiled when I recognized the familiar number, the one that had rung so nonchalantly from time to time many months ago, and then not at all for what seemed like an eternity after the accident. Our greetings were spoken as if nothing had ever interrupted our usual life pattern. It was great to hear his voice again. My wonderful living, loving cousin was making his own rounds, as Dr. Donnelly had done for him throughout his stay in acute care. This follow-up call created the same kind of excitement for me that Donnelly had injected into family and friends during the final days of Preston's stay at FMC. I managed to squeeze a handful of questions into the first few minutes of our conversation, but his answer to my question about his coma is the one that I remember the most.

He told me that sometime during the weeks of his medically induced slumber, he had a dream—more of a scattered reflection, really, some broken thoughts about being interviewed by someone. It was a woman, he said, from the local TV station, asking him all sorts of questions about hunting and an accident, of which he had no memory. She took great interest in details about his hunting partners, the places he had hunted in the past, and the types of guns he had hunted with. "But I couldn't answer her," he told me. "It was so frustrating, why she wanted to know these things, who she was, why she cared," he said. In his dream, he remained confused about the purpose of the interview and unsatisfied that he didn't know the answers to most of her questions. Yet on reflection, he remembered that the interviewer jotted lengthy notes on a legal pad, as if he was providing an extensive answer to each and every question. He recalled becoming so frustrated that he began to cry and demanded that the interviewer stop talking to him. He asked her to quit taking notes and instructed her to go away, which she did. Before she left the room the interviewer politely tilted her head to the side and looked at him as if confused about his annoyance. She touched his shoulder in reassurance of her presence and purpose, and proceeded to fade away.

Dumbfounded by the dream he described, and unsure of how to react to it, I quickly changed the subject. I didn't want Preston to think that I didn't believe what he was telling me, but on the other hand, I wasn't sure why the dream had relevance to our conversation. Was he making the whole dream up? Did *he* even know what he was talking about? Maybe this 'daydreaming' was something that happened to critically ill patients. Maybe I should listen, but revisit the topic with him later, should it remain significant to him in the future.

I directed our discussion towards thoughts about the future-one we could both grasp with enthusiasm now. I asked him about the processes of his lengthy recovery. We talked about Krista and Jackson and how they were coping. We came up with a plan to close out the CaringBridge journal online and recapped how beneficial each of the entries had been to him and his family during his hospitalization. I told him that I had begun living each day with a new appreciation for life, his and my own, and how his accident made me pause and reflect on my blessings rather than focusing on what I felt I'd lost in our relocation from Flagstaff. I told him that, like his family, I was beginning to focus on the future. And I mentioned that it was comforting to be able to settle into a positive place within myself, as I began to appreciate that I was probably just where I was supposed to be, just as I knew he was.

I told him there were things for me yet to learn in my new location, and I promised him that I would stay focused on the possibilities of the future, asking him to do the same. I'd seen the power of remaining positive, especially through the tragedy that he and his family had recently experienced. Appreciation of the little things became more relevant than ever before, we agreed. I reflected with him on the memory of seeing true friends come to his aid with tremendous support and encouragement for the entire month of his hospital stay. We agreed on the significance of good friends.

By this point in our conversation, I was blotting away tears of excitement, trying to keep my voice from revealing that I was crying. I was elated about the fact that he was remembering anything and everything. It was remarkable how focused he sounded. I asked more about his physical wounds, what he was eating, and his goals for the new year. I blurted out question after question as if trying to make up for the time that we'd all lost with him.

He didn't know until months later that I had experienced a journey of my own during his recovery and rehabilitation—a journey to believe in my own future again. I listened carefully to his words of gratitude during the final moments of our phone conversation. Both of us wept openly as we exchanged our thoughts about his unlikely progression to recovery and the impact so many of his supporters had on his monthlong fight for survival. We talked about the CaringBridge site and how it had received more than 8,000 messages of inspiration, and how he would look back and read those messages again from time to time. As we wrapped up our conversation on the phone that morning, we promised each other that we would continue to appreciate more, see each other more often, and carefully guard each moment and memory of our lives moving forward. It was a phone call I will forever remember.

As we agreed on the phone that day, I put together a closing message for followers of CaringBridge as my final update. It was time to close the pages of that chapter of Preston's story. He was ready to take on the new year, and every year, thereafter. My journal entry included the following words, which were written to reassure all the people who had supported and encouraged the Hammonds through the month of December that year.

What began as a way to inform you of updated medical progress and status, continued as an encouraging and uplifting prayer source for Preston and his family, assuring them of your genuine care and concern for our loved one, Preston. It ends happily with a new beginning for Preston, the Hammonds and for each of you. Finally, we can move forward with a new freshness for life through renewed strength and faith, in the power of prayer, and from the goodness of each of you. Sending good wishes for all of you in the new year!

I concluded my message that day with an anonymous quote. The words seemed to talk to me- they summed up the conversation with my cousin that will forever remain close to my heart. My final CaringBridge entry encouraged the journal followers to incorporate the suggestive words of the poem into their lives, as I promised them I would.

As we grow up we learn that even the one person that wasn't supposed to ever let you down, probably will. You will have your heart broken probably more than once and it's harder each time. You'll break hearts too, so remember how it felt when yours was broken.

You'll fight with your best friend. You'll blame a new love for things an old one did.

You'll cry because time is passing too fast, and eventually you'll lose someone you love.

So take too many pictures, laugh too much and love like you've never been hurt. Because every sixty seconds that you spend upset is a minute of happiness you'll never get back.

Don't be afraid that your life will end, be afraid that it will never begin!

CHAPTER 27

Now it was my turn to pay forward the beneficial lessons I had learned from my cousin's healing experience.

Following the example set by my aunt, I reached out to others more in my new environment. I found that putting others' needs before my own helped me feel better too. And I attended church more regularly, something that I had drifted from in recent years. When I reflected on the whys of the accident and the feelings of displacement I had recently struggled with, I could see a pattern woven out of moments and circumstances like puzzle pieces of life that fit together just as they had been intended to. There was purpose to the events of our lives—my cousin's and my own. It wasn't a coincidence that my grandparents had moved to a small town in Arizona so many years ago. That very same community is the one that banded together to support my cousin and his family during their greatest time of need.

Preston's medical transformation and extraordinary recovery prompted him not only to thank all the people and organizations involved in helping him recuperate, but also to reach out to various organizations to help obtain modifications in the systems and procedures to potentially help others experiencing medical emergencies heal successfully too. Preston wasted no time in making sure his accident hadn't happened without a greater purpose. He was following in his dad's footsteps, reaching out to make a positive difference in the lives of others, and it felt wonderful to him to be able to put the accident in a positive perspective. It was one of his chosen ways to show gratitude for his ongoing life.

Less than a year after that fateful day in the forest, his testimonial and photos became the image of the United Blood Service's flyers in Northern Arizona, remaining there for several years. He was interviewed, about his recovery, by a number of organizations, and helped transform his community by inspiring individuals to help others by donating blood. Speaking engagements were arranged at Northern Arizona University on several occasions, where he talked to groups of listeners and spoke about the significance of blood donation, especially in emergency situations, giving examples from his personal experience. He was living proof that community blood drives save lives. His impromptu presentations included details of his accident, which seemed to tug at the heartstrings of his audiences, and raised awareness and blood supply counts throughout northern Arizona.

"Accidents can happen at any time," he would explain, "even when you have years of experience in the outdoors. Thanks to the quick actions of my family, paramedics, doctors, and blood donors, my life was saved. Gratefully, I can still enjoy hunting with my family. That's a tradition that I would like to share with my son."

In addition to inspiring people to donate blood for unforeseen emergencies, Preston was encouraged to bring his extraordinary story of survival to the Arizona State Legislature's House and Senate to help get a bill passed to extend funding for trauma care at hospitals in Northern Arizona. He graciously agreed. He would need to bring a board member from the Flagstaff Medical Center with him, and he would give an account of his story to the Senate and Governor Jan Brewer.

Preston agreed to travel to Phoenix to speak, and decided he wouldn't allow the formal requirements of speaking detour or intimidate him. At first, he wondered what he would say to them. A written speech seemed too formal and would raise his anxiety level—it just wasn't him. And he agreed to meet with board members from the medical center upon his arrival, but he'd also need his own support system, so he brought his brother, Brandon.

Preston's unrehearsed speech, which was more of an outline of the events of November 30, helped increase funding for Flagstaff Medical Center's level I trauma center, which enabled the facility to accommodate emergency situations with advanced teams and technologies, offering the best possible care for patients. As he talked about the events surrounding his accident and rehabilitation at the medical center, he had the undivided attention of the members of the Senate. Concluding his recollection of events, Preston was asked by the governor to reveal, if he didn't mind, who had shot him. Preston unaffectedly motioned to his brother. "This guy did. My brother," he told the governor, as the room's attentiveness gave way to laughter. His plea for assistance came with sincerity and real-life reflection of the need. Preston earned the respect of the Senate that day. Learning about his experience with the Legislator once again reinforced my thoughts about justification of something good stemming from tragedy. His efforts helped to promote the bill that would award Flagstaff Medical Center and other level I trauma centers in Arizona additional funding to help with critical patient situations.

And he didn't stop there.

In his continued quest to regain the lifestyle he once knew and help others do the same, Preston continued advancing mentally and physically in therapy sessions, until he was finally able to return to his regular duties as assistant manager at work. A few months after that, he returned to the forest. It was his intention to live as fully as before, and that meant returning to the outdoor activities that continue to define him today.

Some things changed in regard to the Hammonds' hunts, however. Archery hunting took the place of rifle hunting for a number of years following the accident. Preston's good friend Collin hasn't hunted with Preston for many years, but he sometimes passes the fateful hunting site on his own scouts and hunts. Each time Collin nears the area, he stops near the fence line that the elk trampled that morning just before the shot was fired, and he reflects on gratitude for his best friend. He is grateful as he thinks about how it's still Preston making the cell-phone calls randomly from time to time, in order to meet him in Flagstaff for a round of golf or a craft beer at a local brewery. Its Preston who initiates the get-togethers when he's visiting family in Page. It's Preston who remains the glue that connects them to their past and creates the opportunities for their future experiences.

It was a little more than a year after Preston returned to work when he and two co-workers decided to stop for a cold one on their way home, after work. He had spent the previous nine hours shuffling schedules and monitoring the inventory in lumber at the west-side store. He needed to decompress before calling it a day and he didn't have to twist anyone's arm at the store to join him. After a short walk through the downtown streets of Flagstaff, the three settled at their usual local grub and pub. The restaurant had been a favorite of his, and Krista's, before his accident. It was their 'go-to' desired destination when meeting with friends for appetizers or a burger and karaoke on an occasional Saturday night. Preston hadn't been back since..... everything changed.

The guys agreed on seats at the bar in order to get a better view of the highlights of the previous day's football games on the overhead flat screens. They took turns ordering cold beers and exchanged small talk with the bartender, alternating sips from their frosted mugs. Faintly, out of the corner of his eye, Preston caught a glimpse of a tall brunette with almond-shaped eyes making her way up to the bar beside him to order a drink. Suddenly, his friends' conversations disappeared into the background noise. He leaned over slightly as the attractive woman waited for the bartender to pour her drink and said, "Hey, I recognize you. You're the news reporter, the one on TV."

"No," she assured him, shaking her head. "But that's quite the pick-up line," she added.

"Seriously," Preston responded. "I thought I recognized you from the interview—the tv," he said shaking his head a little, as if his memory was playing tricks on him.

The brunette tilted her head and lifted the corner of her lips to reveal her million-dollar smile. She felt almost sorry for Preston, who seemed to be fumbling in his attempt to meet her. "You must have mistaken me for someone else. I'm not on TV. I'm actually a nurse. My name is Kaelyn."

Preston offered her a handshake. "I'm Preston," he said. "Sorry, I could have sworn that I knew you from somewhere. Great to meet you. Are you sure...?"

"I'm sure," she said, laughing a little as she grabbed her glass of red, turned and walked back toward her table of friends.

CHAPTER 28

As the ongoing months and years continued to fade the memory of the accident, and Preston continued to move forward from it, my curiosity about the circumstances surrounding the incident of November 30, their effects on each of the Hammonds, and the circumstances of Preston's incredible healing process continued to spike. This was especially true every year near the anniversary of it. I sometimes questioned my aunt Camille about some of the specifics, and the way she felt, the month they spent at Flagstaff Medical Center. And she would always recall, with ease, the details and how Preston's story impacted their lives.

I went back to the west-side store in Flagstaff several years ago. Many of the employees and store managers had changed, but the memory of Preston's angel in the rafters remained with some of the personnel. I roamed around the aisles of the store a bit, glancing up at the area where Janelle had told me the angel overlooked the commotion of the store for a number of months that year. I wanted a glimpse of what coworkers might have seen, or an opportunity to feel the energy they may have experienced when they looked up at the mysterious beauty that winter. I wanted to know if there were any traces of her presence in the electrical department. Nothing.

I snapped a few pictures and walked out of the store feeling a bit disappointed, like I'd missed a significant sign from above. I wished I had been aware of her the year of her existence. I concluded that her presence had served a comforting purpose for the employees who knew about her, and once again I would have to rely on the mention of her occurrence in my aunt's journal on the day the store manager visited following the Christmas party. I found it odd that aunt Camille hadn't mentioned the angel much in recent years, nor had she ever shared the note about her or any details about her occurrence until I decided to write Preston's story.

During our conversations recollecting the days and nights at the medical center that winter, I asked about the mystery of the angel's appearance and about Camille's interpretation of her meaning. She hadn't been aware of the angel in the west-side store either, she told me, until Gary mentioned it. Understandably, her efforts had been focused on remaining close to my cousin and her family during those turbulent months. But knowing my aunt, she'd have focused strictly on the power of prayer and her faith during that time anyway. She was notably appreciative of assisting angels—the one in the store's rafters and the one she had spoken to accompanying the car-accident patient in the emergency room that one night. Her Catholic upbringing allowed her to appreciate the significance of symbolic signs from heaven, but she wasn't star-struck and didn't feel she'd been deprived of anything by not seeing the angel herself. She told me that she concluded that the purpose of angels being placed around her that December was to assure her not to be afraid. If that was indeed their intention, they accomplished that goal.

I've held onto the miracle for a little more than a decade now. I'm not sure if it's the return of hunting season or the Thanksgiving holiday that causes me to reflect, but with each passing November and each return of chill to the early morning air, my thoughts go back to the season that forever changed the life of my cousin and the one when I regained my trust in faith. With help from observing Preston's miraculous medical ordeal, I overcame obstacles and hurdles in my own struggle to believe again. I had always trusted that God existed, but never accepted the power of trusting His plan for me—for all of us. Finally, I am practicing the perseverance and commitment to faith that the Hammonds have continually displayed through the years.

Preston was granted a second chance at life that he is openly grateful for to this day. It has been a decade since that fateful day, the day my cousin's life was changed in numerous ways. Today, the hunter who was critically injured in an accident near Flagstaff is a more gracious person, continually vowing to live in the current moment. He has a fresh appreciation for his family and friends and for those who helped him through a season he has little recollection of. His two-and-a-half-week coma caused him not only to pause physically from his life of youth and adventure, but also to pause mentally, so that he might better appreciate and reflect upon his gifts of family, friendship, and his ability to conquer obstacles. Over the past decade, his son, Jackson, has matured into his favorite scholar, sports performer, fishing partner, and fellow outdoorsman.

An additional hardship occurred during Preston's rehabilitation. The stress of the accident and the complicated things that can happen during a young marriage with turbulent twists and turns became more than two young adults could withstand. Preston's marriage to Krista sadly ended, but he found love again with his soul mate—the woman from his comatose dream, Kaelyn. He continues to struggle with some short-term memory loss, even a decade later, but considers himself mentally and physically 95 percent recovered again.

Five years after returning to the Flagstaff west-side Home Depot, Preston was promoted to store manager and was transferred to another Arizona location. It was an advancement he'd worked toward prior to the accident-one he'd attended training preparations for weeks before the fateful hunt.

Today, Preston and Kaelyn, along with their children, have blended a family and a simple lifestyle they share together, nestled in a quiet mountain town that they call home. The gracefulness of the wilderness continues to radiate in my cousin, and the charm of their life in the mountains serves as the perfect platform to allow their future chapters to gently unfold.

"The best way I can describe Preston is, he was as close to being dead as you can be, but still alive. It's just a delight to see how he's returned to his normal life. I am surprised, and sometimes I have to pinch myself a little bit."

—Dr. Mark Donnelly

EPILOGUE

A couple of months before I began to pull the pieces of Preston's story together, I was sitting next to him at Thanksgiving dinner, at a gigantic oval dining table in a lodge our family had rented in the White Mountains. The past ten years had distanced everyone who was gathered there for the holiday, a world away from where we'd been sitting a decade earlier. After placing a heaping mound of mashed potatoes next to a slice of turkey on my plate, I passed the serving bowl to my cousin and noticed his face was overcome with emotion. I didn't have to ask why he was crying; every one of us gathered around the table knew the exact reason. It was nearing the anniversary of the day in the forest when his life was almost taken. Seeing him emotionally broken that holiday was the final push of motivation I needed to set aside my reluctance about writing a book and start putting the events of his accident into tangible pages. His could be a story shared with others close to him for years to come. Without a doubt, it's one worth telling. Writing it would be my way of honoring his bravery and determination, a celebration of sorts for the season when he overcame the unimaginable, through the support of many and through the grace of God.

During the process of putting the circumstances surrounding Preston's accident into words, I spent a significant amount of time discussing the events that took place on and around that fateful November day with my cousins and my aunt and uncle. Many of our conversations included recollections of the details surrounding the accident. Although it has been a long time since that tragic day in the forest that nearly claimed Preston's life, the scars in his family's memories have not faded. I cannot count the number of times that Uncle Brian's voice broke into silence as we replayed the actions of those critical moments. Repeatedly, Brian would conclude a thought with, "And that saved his life."

I'm indebted to my cousin and his family for answering my phone calls and text messages at random times of the day and night, helping me gather information for his story over the course of the past year. I'm appreciative of their support in helping me get in touch with some people that helped shape his story, in any way they could. The Hammonds have expressed that they remain forever thankful to those who assisted in Preston's recovery: the professionals at the Summit fire station, the ambulance drivers, and the police officers and detectives who were first responders that cold November day. They are eternally grateful to the surgeons, doctors, nurses, and therapists. They'll always be thankful to the members of their church, family and friends, coworkers and community—everyone who played a significant role in Preston's recovery. Ten years later, my aunt and uncle still send Christmas cards expressing appreciation for their connections with many of the heroes who helped save Preston's life. But if you knew my aunt and uncle, these gestures of appreciation wouldn't surprise you. Once you've become a friend of the Hammonds, you're a friend for life.

For many months, as I wrote and rewrote, our phone conversations concluded with recollections of some incredible parts of his story—some I hadn't known until I dug into medical reports and my aunt's journal. We concluded time and time again that it was a combination of efforts and circumstances that saved my cousin:

- Uncle Brian's past EMT training, which taught him to lay a bleeding victim wound-side down for transport—that saved his life.
- The cold temperature in the forest that morning that slowed his blood flow and kept his body temperature down—that saved his life.
- The unlikely presence of a paramedic at the Summit fire station who could intercept and start an IV before ambulance transport to the hospital—that saved his life.
- The coincidence of a cardiac anesthesiologist, James Delgaria, being on duty the day Preston arrived in the emergency room—that saved his life.
- The (possible) deflection of the bullet by a tree into Preston's wrist, slowing its speed through his chest—that saved his life.
- The fact that the bullet did not explode within him or exit his body—that saved his life.
- The meticulous surgical hands of Dr. Donnelly during the first crucial hours after the accident—that saved his life.
- The kidney dialysis machine newly installed at Flagstaff Medical Center—that saved his life.
- The loving support and continual encouragement of his Home Depot coworkers, —that saved his life.
- The presence of the woman, now believed to be an angel, in the FMC hallway, and the angel in the Home Depot rafters that provided a measure of calmness to Preston's supporters—that saved his life.
- Most important, the power and plan of God, answering prayers for healing from family and friends—that saved his life.

While gathering information and reflecting on the events of the accident with the trauma surgeon, Mark Donnelly, MD, FACS, he told me about something that happened to him at the Home Depot a significant amount of time after the accident. As he began to describe his encounter at the west-side store, I anticipated that he might reference something about the presence of angel in the rafters. Instead, he told me about the admiration employees had maintained for Preston for years following the accident. He laughed a little as he recalled an outing to purchase a bucket full of sawdust for his compost development process at home. He told me that the person helping him at the store that day wasn't enthused about his request to scoop up the loose sawdust from beneath the boards and electric saws in the lumber area, and even discouraged this request. During their discussion, another employee walked past them, and turned back to get a better look at Dr. Donnelly. "Aren't you the doctor that took care of Preston Hammond?" he asked, recognizing him from his visits to the hospital. "Yes, I am," said Donnelly. Suddenly, his request was honored, and a *truckload* of sawdust was quickly obtained.

Dr. Donnelly expressed that although he doesn't consider himself "the most religious person," he does believe in God and also believes that God has intervened and become "involved" several times in his life, one of those interventions came to him during the time Preston was under his care. A few of those nudges from above prompted him to proceed with caution—a reminder that he might not always readily have the most accurate answers. In Preston's case, however, he agrees that the intervening seemed to be more of a pat on the back than a cautious nudge.

Sure, there are still days, many of them, when the validity of my own faith is tested. True faith—it's the real deal. I've found that it's going to take the opportunity occasionally to shake you to your core. It's tested me that way. It's going to create opportunity for complete denial; it's going to leave you feeling confused, doubt-ful, angry, and broken. And when this happens, you're going to question your reasons for ever believing at all. But, after the dust of tragedy settles, it is the good things that come from these mis-fortunes, the people who come together as a result of those ter-rible moments, that affect your perspective about faith and give you reason to believe. It's the positive gestures that rise above the negative ones. That's what I remind myself when those trials in life appear. That's where the ray of sunshine raises me from the darkness of doubt. That's when my faith prevails. It's happened for me time and time again. For me, it was reflecting on my cousin and his family and the unwavering measures of belief and trust they displayed during their darkest days that help me continually readjust my focus.

And, of course, there are days like this one, when I remember "the miracle." That's when I feel like everything in life is in align-ment. It is on a day like this when leaning on faith comes easy and feels comforting and rewarding. Maybe that confidence is partly due to the way that, after a struggle, life returns—as it did for my cousin—and the world seems in perfect balance. Or possibly I'm being rewarded with another gracious occasional blessing. Either way, I'm grateful that I more easily recognize the purpose of hard-ships and blessings—often, they go hand-in-hand. Maybe there is a possibility that I've grown enough spiritually over the past de-cade to accept the fact that every circumstance has a greater pur-pose, if only I am patient enough to allow myself to experience its meaning.

Having faith has helped me to forgive myself for my reluctanc-es, my flaws, and my past mistakes, and it has also given me the courage to pour out my thoughts on Preston's recovery endlessly on paper. It is days like these when the words flow from my mind, down through my fingertips, and begin an energetic tap dance on my keyboard. It is days like this when I am able to remember, with ease, the events and circumstances that brought my cousin (and me) back to a greater understanding of this life.

"I want to live every day to the fullest. That doesn't mean going skydiving or anything like that, but I'm going to continue to do the same things as before. I just want to enjoy them even more now."

—Preston Hammond

Made in the USA
San Bernardino, CA
17 February 2018